Augusta

LIFE, LOVE AND FOOD

Augusta
Life, Love and Food

From Paiágua to
Priors Hardwick

Foreword by Baroness Knight of Collingtree DBE

Live Wire Books

First published in 2007 for Lino and Augusta Pires by
Live Wire Books, The Orchard, School Lane,
Warmington, Banbury, Oxfordshire, OX17 1DE
T   01295 690624   F   01295 690358

www.livewirebooks.com
info@livewirebooks.com

Further copies of this book can be obtained from
The Butcher's Arms, Priors Hardwick, Southam,
Warwickshire, CV47 7SN.
Price £20 plus £2.50 p&p
T   01327 260504.
www.thebutchersarms.com.
enquiries@thebutchersarms.com

ISBN 978-0-9553124-2-7

A catalogue record for this book is available
from the British Library

Designed by Andrew Barron @ thextension
Picture Research by Jill Todd and Andrew Barron

Printed and bound in Dubai by Oriental Press

Contents

Foreword

If anyone asked me to name a lady as a role model for a perfect wife, I would, without hesitation, suggest Augusta.

Young Lino, aged about eleven at the time, showed astonishingly good judgement when he fell in love with the pretty little girl who sat near him in the schoolroom and made up his mind to marry her. I am not sure whether their parents entirely approved, but the couple did, indeed, marry as soon as they could after leaving school and from then on Augusta's whole life has been devoted to loving, supporting, encouraging and helping her husband, whatever the cost to herself.

What a leap in the dark it must have been, back in the fifties, for the shy young lady who had never in her life travelled far from her home in a distant mountain village in Portugal, to leave her family and the world she grew up in, to go to a strange land, to do a job which was new to her, with people she knew only slightly. She knew neither their customs nor more than a few words of their language, but she did know that the move would give her husband his chance. She did not hesitate.

In the years that have followed, huge difficulties have been faced and overcome. There must have been many times when Augusta despaired. Like the time when she first saw the kitchen of *The Butcher's Arms* – how on earth was she to prepare good and healthy meals in such a cramped space, with grease and dirt congealed on every surface and no proper ovens or cold stores? But Augusta is not the frail, helpless and emotional woman she may sometimes seem to be. She did, indeed, burst into tears, but they were soon dried and her steely, brave, 'let's get on with it, then' character took over.

Thousands of diners would testify that *The Butcher's Arms* of today is far more than a superb restaurant in a beautiful garden. Whenever we go, we are warmly welcomed and served a sumptuous meal by a beautifully drilled staff. Few realise how much is owed to Augusta. She attends to every detail; she has taught the chefs to cook and the staff to serve.

Even when her health has let her down, she has never for one moment let her husband down. I offer her my affectionate salute. What a woman!

Baroness Knight of Collingtree, DBE

Prologue

IF YOU DON'T KNOW IT ALREADY THEN YOU
CERTAINLY SHOULD DO BY THE TIME YOU HAVE
READ THROUGH THIS BOOK: MY MOTHER IS A
TRULY REMARKABLE WOMAN.

From the humblest of beginnings, she and my father, together, have managed to achieve more in their lives than would ever have seemed possible when they were growing up in the back of beyond in Portugal all those years ago – and Dad would be the first to tell you that much of the credit for their extraordinary success must go to Mum.

She may not be such a showman as he is – which is probably just as well, or Sunday lunch at *The Butcher's Arms* would be more like Sunday Night at The Palladium! Even in her supporting role, she shies away from the limelight. And yet, behind the scenes, her contribution has been absolutely vital. In so many ways, but especially through her skills in the kitchen and her inexhaustible capacity for hard work, which has always gone way beyond the call of duty, she has been largely responsible for bringing my father's most ambitious schemes to fruition and for helping to make all his wildest dreams of business success come true.

We have had a succession of very talented head chefs at *The Butcher's Arms*, but Augusta taught each one of them just about everything they know – and I think that all of them would probably admit that she still has the edge over them. As well as masterminding the kitchen, developing the menus, doing all the fresh flower arrangements in the dining room, supervising the laying up of the tables, keeping the staff on their toes and generally ensuring that the restaurant runs smoothly, she also manages to keep Dad and me in order. And, somehow, she makes it all look effortless.

As well as her enormous contribution to the success of *The Butcher's Arms*, she has much else to be proud of. For instance, her skills as a needlewoman are unsurpassed and quite breathtaking, as anyone who has had the opportunity to admire her crochet and embroidery work will tell you. And her green-fingered gardening has drawn high praise from one of the country's leading professionals.

More than some who have claimed the title, Mum really is Superwoman.

Despite all this, she remains down-to-earth, modest and self-effacing to a fault. These qualities, along with her kindness, generosity and gentle concern for others are what have endeared her to generations of *Butcher's Arms* customers, as is made abundantly clear by the many affectionate tributes and reminiscences included in this book.

Her naturally maternal instincts are well known to anyone who has ever arrived at *The Butcher's Arms* with a small child, only to have Mum sweep the infant into her arms and disappear with it, leaving the parents to enjoy a peaceful lunch or dinner.

Needless to say, I was spoilt rotten as a child by the most loving of mums. She was always there for me. And yet I know that she fretted endlessly about the difficulty of balancing a punishing work schedule with home and family life and the decision to send me off to boarding school was very difficult for her. She needn't have worried – I had a great time. For one thing, there were more girls at Rugby than in Priors Hardwick!

Everyone who has ever come into contact with Mum will know what a huge-hearted person she is. On the surface, she always has been a big softie, dissolving into tears at the slightest provocation. But underneath all that she is an immensely strong character, as has been demonstrated over the last few years by the way in which she has come through what have been some really awful times health-wise for her, for Dad and for me.

As a wife, business partner, mother and grandmother, Augusta is very special. As well as being a celebration of her Golden Wedding anniversary, this book is the family's way of saying: "Thanks for everything".

Peter Pires
APRIL 2007

The chapel clock in Paiágua as it looks today.

Part One

Paiágua

The sound of the chapel clock in Paiágua striking the hour is enough to reduce Augusta to tears of nostalgia.

Nearly fifty years after she moved away, those familiar chimes – occasionally overheard in the background during long-distance telephone conversations with relatives who still live in the village – bring vivid childhood memories flooding back. The reason it has such a powerful effect on her is that when Augusta was growing up in the 1930s and 1940s, nobody in Paiágua possessed clocks or watches; out in the fields, people told the time by the sun, while the chiming of the chapel clock regulated the entire village's daily routine.

Portugal in those days was one of the poorest and most backward countries in Western Europe and in the more remote peasant communities such as Paiágua – located two hundred miles north east of Lisbon, in the beautiful, mountainous Beira Baixa region – life could be very hard indeed. There was no electricity, no running water and no services of any kind and with very few proper roads and no access to radio or regular daily newspapers, people living out in the sticks were effectively cut off from the rest of the world. Augusta was twelve years old before she made her first visit to the nearest big town, Castelo Branco. And it was only then that she saw electric lights for the first time in her life. Such modern conveniences were unknown in Paiágua, where the houses, some of them little more than hovels, were dimly lit by candles and oil lamps.

Many of those in the tight-knit little community, especially among the older

Castelo Branco as it must have looked to Augusta
when first she visited at the age of twelve.

generation, had never ventured further afield than neighbouring hamlets and villages. Most people were self-sufficient on a subsistence level as far as food was concerned, while necessities such as paraffin for lamps and minor luxuries such as sugar, tea and coffee were available from the village taverna, which was kept by one of Augusta's uncles. Other needs were catered for by individual craftsmen living in the village – the local carpenter, blacksmith, stonemason, shoemaker and dressmaker, most of whom operated part-time, as and when required. Medical facilities were extremely basic. In an emergency, a doctor could be summoned from Castelo Branco, but with most minor complaints nature would be left to take its course. Or traditional herbal remedies might be used. The village barber doubled as a dentist, pulling teeth with a pair of pliers – and no anaesthetic!

Augusta, the fifth of Manuel and Maria Marques's six children, was born in 1934 – not in August as her name suggests, but in October. It was the tradition in Portugal in those days for children to be named after their Godparents. Augusta's Godmother was called Maria – but so were both her mother and her elder sister. Her Godfather was Augusto, so she became Augusta. Matters were then further complicated when her younger sister was also named Maria. She became known as Mario Santos and her elder sister as Maria Marques in an effort to avoid confusion. The truth is that if you called out the name Maria in the square, half the women and girls in the village would answer!

Augusta's father was a respected man in the village, brought in as the 'money counter' to help broker any business dealings between villagers and also called upon to settle any small disputes. As well as having quite a bit of land in and around the village, he was also the local builder so the family were regarded as being comfortably off. Even so,

Maria Santos (Augusta's younger sister)

. . . .

❛ Augusta and I not only shared a bedroom, we also shared a small single bed.
I really enjoyed her company most of the time, but in winter there
was a problem because she had such cold feet and she'd deliberately put
them next to mine, which I hated.

Like most of the children in Paiágua, we didn't have toys to play with.
We never had real dolls or a dolls' house so we would make pretend ones out of
stones. We cooked imaginary caldo verde (cabbage
soup), which was what everybody lived on most of the
time, using the terracotta bowls in which pine resin
was collected as bowls and flat stones as plates. The
boys used to play football with a ball made from a
piece of leftover cloth stuffed with rags. We would
sometimes join in. Our brother, Francisco, would
build toy cars from pieces of wood with the lids
from shoe wax tins as wheels. ❜

. . . .

Augusta at seventeen with, inset, older sister Maria Marques
fetching water from a tap in the square after mains water
was supplied to Paiágua for the first time in the 1960s.

their lifestyle was fairly basic. Their house, in a narrow street that was actually no more than a stony path just off the village square, was built of mud and stone in the traditional manner and consisted of just one main living room, with two small bedrooms upstairs and a windowless basement below. There wasn't even a proper outside toilet, let alone an indoor one. You simply crouched behind the wall or retreated into a corner of the lean-to where the goats were kept. The large leaves from corn cobs served as toilet paper.

Manuel and his wife slept in the basement, which also served as a storeroom for fruit and vegetables, the couple's bed set up among sacks of beans, maize and potatoes and large terracotta amphorae full of chorizo and olives preserved in either salt or oil. Augusta and her younger sister, Maria Santos, shared a bed in one of the tiny upstairs bedrooms while their older brothers, Jose and Francisco, slept in the other. Until their two much older sisters, Maria Marques and Delfina, got married and moved out, the place was even more crowded.

The living room, sparsely furnished with a table and a few rough wooden chairs, included a kitchen area at one end. Most of the cooking would be done in a large pot suspended over the open fire or on a sheet of tin placed over the embers to serve as a griddle. Bread made from flour ground on the village's communal, water-driven mill would be baked in the communal village oven. On special occasions, such as fiestas, saints' days and weddings, meat might also be roasted in the same big oven just off the square – the bread at the back, the meat, along with potatoes, onions and peppers, on the embers raked forward to the front.

People dressed simply in clothes that were often home made. Her mother always wore black, with a headscarf, while her father lived in hard-wearing dark brown trousers,

Most of the cooking would be done in a large pot
suspended over the open fire (top). The communal village oven (bottom) seen today –
full of weeds and debris.

*Augusta with her family, her parents Manuel and Maria
at the front with behind (l to r) Francisco, Augusta, Jose,
Maria Marques, Delfina and Maria Santos.*

coarse linen shirts and work boots made from old rubber car tyres. He had one rather shapeless suit for special occasions. The linen for his shirts came from the raw flax that was grown down by the river and that the women in the family then spun and wove on their own loom. Augusta preferred bright colours. She started making her own dresses and blouses when she was still very young, using cloth bought either on rare visits to Castelo Branco or from a travelling salesman who would come to the village from time to time, selling from a horse-drawn cart. At other times, clothes would be run up for her either by her sister, Delfina, or by a cousin in Paiágua, both skilled dressmakers.

The normal daily routine was always the same. First thing each morning, Augusta's mother would light the fire and fetch water from the well before rousing the rest of the family at around 5.30am. Breakfast would almost invariably be a vegetable broth of some kind. On chilly winter mornings, the younger members of the family would huddle together around the flames, perched on the stone hearth surround while they ate. Then, after taking turns to splash cold water on their faces, everybody would set off to work on the family's few scattered acres. Augusta's father rode everywhere on a donkey. The younger children would have chores to do around the house before going to school, which they attended only between the ages of seven and ten. At all other times they would be out in the fields with the rest of the family.

This would sometimes involve walking for over an hour just to get to the more distant, outlying plots high up on the surrounding hillsides where the family owned an olive grove, an orchard and a small vineyard, producing their own olive oil and also their own wine, the children treading the grapes in a big wooden tub. Down in the valley, on the

*Everything in the fields had to be done by hand
and the whole family would join in with the ploughing,
digging, planting, weeding and hoeing.*

fertile land along the shallow, fast-flowing riverside, they grew all kinds of vegetables, along with maize, wheat, rye and flax. The flax would be spun and woven into linen by the womenfolk and then made into sheets, pillow cases and tablecloths as well as clothing. The family also kept a herd of around forty goats, a few chickens and, like everyone else in the village, a couple of pigs that would be slaughtered to provide the household with meat throughout the year.

Children grew up fast in this tough environment and by the age of six Augusta was already part of the family workforce. One of her earliest memories is of being sent off on her own with a basket of lettuce seedlings that had to be planted out in a field quite some distance away. She vividly remembers walking for what seemed like miles, terrified of getting lost, especially when she found herself wandering through a rather spooky area where the narrow path was enclosed on each side by tall reeds. By the time she eventually arrived at her destination she was in tears.

She was also expected to do her fair share of jobs around the house from a very early age. Once a week, the place would be thoroughly cleaned from top to bottom. Instead of a scrubbing brush you had to use handfuls of a coarse, gorse-like plant that scratched your fingers painfully. Other tasks that fell to the more junior members of any family included collecting heather on which to bed the animals down, while the roots would be burned to make charcoal. The girls would also have to help their mothers with the laundry. This was done on an area of flat rock down by the river, using home-made soap, after which it would be laid out in the sun to dry. It would then be pressed using an iron heated with charcoal.

In the little single-room schoolhouse, presided over by Professora Cutilda Silva Cardoso, the village children learned to read and write, something that most of the older generation, including Augusta's mother, were quite unable to do. They were also taught some basic arithmetic and a little bit of history. Paper of any sort being in very short supply, the children would write on slate, using chalk.

Augusta was a bright little girl, but as soon as she left school at ten she went back to working full-time on the family's land. For a while, she was given the job of looking after the goats. Every morning she would walk them out to the hillside grazing pastures, quite some distance away, and would then stay with them all day long, knitting socks for her father and her brothers while she watched over them.

As she got older, the workload got heavier. Everything in the fields had to be done by hand and the whole family would join in with the ploughing, digging, planting, weeding, hoeing, watering and harvesting. And when they weren't busy on their own land, they would earn a few extra escudos by taking seasonal jobs as casual labourers on large farms in the region. When she was sixteen, Augusta joined other villagers who went to help with the olive harvest on an estate near Castelo Branco. She would go for the week, taking her own food with her and sleeping in a makeshift dormitory in a barn.

The olive harvest at home was one of the jobs that Augusta dreaded most of all. This took place in November. The olive grove was located some miles away, up in the mountains, and the family would set out before dawn to walk there, taking turns to hitch rides in the ox cart. At that time of year it would often be freezing cold up on the exposed slopes. And to make matters worse, the track leading back to the village happened to run along the top of the slope, meaning that each basketful of olives had to be carried uphill to the waiting ox cart, the basket balanced on one's head.

Like all the other girls in the village, Augusta had mastered this art at a very early age, learning to carry not just baskets but also quite heavy earthenware pots full of water on her head, using a special padded ring to support the weight. Examples of these rings can be seen on display in the bar at *The Butcher's Arms*, a constant reminder to Augusta of just how far she has come since those days. At the same time, she insists that it was all those years of fetching and carrying water from the well in this way that explains why, to this very day, she still has such perfect, straight-backed posture. So, something good did come from it! It was out of the same sort of sheer necessity that she also learned other, more useful skills that were to serve her well over the years, although not in ways that she could possibly have envisaged at the time.

For women, generally, the traditional way of life in the villages was extremely

Jose da Silva (Husband of Augusta's cousin, Maria da Graca):

....

'Augusta and I used to go to school together. When we were in the third year class we had a new teacher who turned out to suffer from epilepsy. One day she had a fit and fell off her chair. We were all so terrified that we ran out of the room — some went through the door and others jumped out of the window in their haste to get out. After that, it was explained to us what epilepsy was and from then on Augusta and the rest of us would help the teacher when she had an attack. We would tie her to the chair with a cloth! '

....

*The olive grove was located some miles away, up in the mountains, and the family would
set out before dawn to walk there, taking turns to hitch rides in the ox cart.*

demanding, an endless round of drudgery and toil, with regular child-bearing thrown in
for good measure. As well as having to look after what were often very large families, wives
were also expected to do their full share of backbreaking labour in the fields, while at the
same time making sure that their cramped, overcrowded homes were kept clean and tidy.
On top of all that, they had to make a lot of their own clothes and were expected to find
ways of preparing nourishing meals out of a limited range of home-grown ingredients.

Augusta's mother was a particularly good cook and it was at her knee that she
learned the basic skills that were to stand her in such good stead in the early days of *The
Butcher's Arms* when, despite having had no formal training whatsoever, she took over the
kitchen with such success that the pub's reputation for great home-cooked food soon
spread far and wide. And although the menu has, of course, become more sophisticated
and very much more extensive over the years, Augusta's influence is still much in evidence.

For instance, the Portuguese rice pudding that remains such a great favourite on the sweet trolley is made to the same recipe that was passed down to her by her mum.

"I remember her cooking it in a big copper pot suspended over the fire," recalls Augusta, savouring the memory. "Some of it would get stuck on the bottom and I always begged her to allow me scrape the pot. It was always lovely and sweet and sticky."

Soup was the staple diet for the family during the week, but there would occasionally be something special on a Sunday, maybe goat or chicken casserole, or ham. Most families kept a pig or two that would be fattened up ready for slaughter just before Christmas.

"We never grew attached to the pig – it wasn't like having a pet," insists Augusta, adding: "There was one particular man in the village who would always be called in to do the killing for everybody. There would be great excitement on the day and we would all gather round to watch. Looking back, it was rather gruesome, but it didn't seem to bother us, even when they held a bucket under the neck to catch the blood. In those days, it was all about survival and you didn't think twice about it. But I couldn't watch it now. I would find it much too upsetting."

Once the pig had been killed, the bristles would be singed off with a lighted taper and the carcass would then be butchered and the various different joints and cuts prepared and preserved, a process that would involve a weekend of frantic activity in the kitchen. The legs and shoulders would be smoked over the fire and then hung from the rafters, while the rest of the meat would be made into sausages. Nothing would be allowed to go to waste. The intestines would be washed in the river and then made into chorizo, a type of sausage spiced with cumin and paprika, the bones would be boiled for stock and even the blood would be saved and used for black pudding. The occasion would then be celebrated with a feast at which all those parts of the animal that couldn't be preserved in some way or another would be eaten.

None of the houses had their own ovens. Everybody used the communal one just off the main village square – a vast clay oven that was heated by a wood fire. The villagers also shared an olive press, which was maintained and looked after by Augusta's father, and a small, water-driven flour mill. Augusta's mother would bake bread and cakes once-a-week in the communal oven, using flour milled from the family's own wheat. "As a young girl, I would watch her kneading the dough and I was always desperate to get my hands on it, but it was only when I was much older that she used to let me help her," recalls Augusta.

Thinking back, she adds: "One of the greatest treats as far as I was concerned was being able to dip her fresh-baked bread, still warm from the oven, into our own olive oil. Absolutely delicious! It made all the hard work that went into picking the olives seem worthwhile."

Any spare time that the womenfolk might have would be spent spinning, weaving, sewing and embroidering. Augusta's sister, Delfina, was an expert dressmaker and owned a rather ancient pedal-operated sewing machine on which she would make clothes for herself and the rest of the family. As a child, Augusta was desperate to start sewing herself and would beg to be allowed to help with buttonholes and hems. She learned quickly and had mastered the basics by the age of eight. Two years later, when Delfina got married and moved away, Augusta started making her own clothes.

The villagers also shared an olive press (top) and a small,
wooden flour grinder (bottom).

She soon developed other needlework skills. A woman from Paiágua, who had
gone away to live in France for some years, returned to the village just before the war and
taught all the girls how to knit, after which Augusta knitted baby clothes for her little
nephew, José. At the same time, a cousin gave her a pattern to crochet and she walked
miles to a neighbouring village to buy cotton, using it to crochet small table mats. Her
mother was concerned about spending even the small amount of money that this cost, but
her father, normally a very strict man, indulged her. "If she wants to, let her do it," he said.
At around the same time, one of her sisters-in-law taught her how to embroider and
she would practice on pieces of linen that she got from her grandmother. She still has
the first sample she ever did, when she was fourteen.

It was impossible to do embroidery or crochet work by the dim light of candles and
oil lamps, so after dark on winter evenings Augusta, her mother and her sisters would sit
and spin the flax that the family grew down by the river and which they would eventually
weave into linen cloth on the old hand-made loom that had been set up in a hayloft in the
yard outside.

The process of producing linen from raw flax was long and laborious. The flax
would be harvested in May and, once the seeds had been removed to make linseed oil, the
plants themselves would be left to soak in the river for a week before being laid out on the
bank to dry in the sun. Next, they would be put through a sort of threshing procedure in
which they would first be beaten flat with mallets and then drawn through a piece of
equipment known as a tasker to separate the fibres, which at this stage would look like long
hairs and would feel dry and crackly. After being smoothed and combed, these fibres would

then be spun into yarn by hand, patiently and painstakingly twisted around the fingers.

Augusta can remember how, from September onwards, almost every evening would be spent sitting around the fire in the candlelight, spinning in this way – and gossiping all the while.

The final stage in the process involved coating the thread in a mixture of ash and water to give it that special heavyweight linen texture and it would then be woven on the loom. You would end up with two types of linen, one fine and one coarse. The fine grade would be used to make linen shirts for the men as well as sheets and pillow cases, the pillow cases stuffed with the shredded leaves stripped from corn-on-the-cob. The coarser grade would be used for bedspreads, tablecloths and cushion covers.

By the time she was sixteen, Augusta had added the art of weaving to her other needlework skills and was starting to produce the most beautiful pieces of embroidered and crocheted lace linenware. Not only has she never forgotten these skills; she has actually developed and perfected them, providing herself with a hobby that has given her enormous pleasure and quiet satisfaction throughout her life.

Like many village girls of her generation, Augusta may have dreamed of breaking free from the restrictions of traditional village life as she sat there spinning by candlelight, but at that time her horizons would still have been severely limited. The height of her ambition would probably have been to marry well and maybe get the chance to move away to Lisbon or any other big town that could offer the prospect of a brighter future. And that was about as far as it went.

For any girl in Augusta's situation, the first priority was to find the right man.

Paiágua as it is today.

Augusta's family olive groves are up on the horizon, at the point where there is a dip in the line of hills.

Caldo Verde
PORTUGUESE GREEN SOUP

This is a classic Portuguese dish. It is the simple, nutritious soup that my mother would make in the three legged pot hanging over the open fire in our home in Paiágua. The Portuguese soups tend to be hearty affairs. They had to be, they had to keep us going for hours, working in the fields.

MAKES ONE LARGE POT

2 large onions, finely chopped

4 cloves garlic, crushed

4 tablespoons olive oil

1 chorizo sausage (optional)

6 large potatoes, peeled and sliced

1.5 litres/2½ pints good vegetable or chicken stock

2 bay leaves

large bunch of greens – cabbage or kale – finely chopped

salt and freshly ground black pepper, to taste

Sweat the onions and garlic in the olive oil until translucent. Chop the sausage, if using, into small chunks and add to the onion. Sweat the onion, garlic and sausage for a few more minutes and then add the diced potatoes.

Transfer the mixture to a large pan, add the stock, seasoning and bay leaves and cook until the potatoes are soft.

When the potatoes are ready, mash them into the broth to make a thick base.

Blanch the greens in boiling water for one minute to take off any bitterness, drain, then add to the broth. Add as much cabbage as you can get into the broth. If you want a heavy soup add a lot of greens. If you prefer to lighter soup, add less.

Simmer for a few minutes.

Goat Stew

Meat was rarely available, apart from the pork we would eat in November when the pig was killed. But many people in Paiágua enjoyed this tasty goat stew on special occasions or fiesta days.

We cooked it in terracotta pots in the village communal oven. My sister Maria has her own clay oven in her house, which she heats with a fire. She still makes this recipe, it's delicious.

SERVES 4

2 lbs/1 kilo goat meat cut into chunks

3 tablespoons olive oil

2 onions, finely chopped

2 garlic cloves, crushed

½ pint/300ml of wine (we used our own home made rosé wine)

(add more water or beef stock if it is too dry)

few sprigs of thyme

1 bay leaf

salt and pepper

Heat the oil and fry the meat for a few minutes to brown it. Add the onions and garlic and sauté until translucent. Add wine, water or stock, thyme, bay leaf, salt and pepper. Cook in a slow oven for an hour and a half, or until the meat is tender

Tejelada

Few people outside of Portugal know that the Portuguese love desserts, cakes and pastries. Every fiesta day we would make this wonderful pudding, which is similar to crème caramel. We always cooked it in terracotta pots and put in the communal village oven.

SERVES 6–8
1 pint of milk
6 eggs
6 flat tablespoons of sugar
1 heaped tablespoon of plain flour
1 teaspoon of cinnamon
grated zest of one lemon
pinch of salt

Beat the eggs and gradually add the flour. Beat in the sugar and milk. Add the salt, cinnamon and zest of lemon. Mix well. Pour the mixture into a baking dish and place in a hot oven for an hour.

The prettiest girl in the village – for Lino it was love at first sight.

Part Two

Lino

LIFTING THE LID OF HER DESK IN THE LITTLE SCHOOLROOM AT PAIÁGUA ONE MORNING, AUGUSTA WAS SURPRISED TO DISCOVER A SCRAP OF LINED PAPER ON WHICH A BRIEF NOTE HAD BEEN SCRIBBLED IN PENCIL.

Stifling a giggle, she blushed scarlet as she read through what turned out to be a declaration of undying love from classmate Lino Pires. She was the prettiest girl in the village, he wrote, and went on to ask if she would agree to be his girlfriend.

Augusta was just ten at the time and Lino little more than a year older, so the note, which she hurriedly and surreptitiously folded and slipped into her pocket, was little more than an expression of innocent puppy love. And yet it marked the beginning of a romance that was to last a lifetime.

As it happened, Augusta had already developed a bit of soft spot for Lino before he sent that first love letter. The son of poor peasant farmer from the neighbouring hamlet of Vinha, which lay two miles away on the other side of the valley, he was the only youngster from that tiny, outlying community who attended the school in Paiágua. In fact, he was the first person from among the nine families living in Vinha who had ever learned to read and write. It was only later that Augusta found out that it was Lino himself who had insisted on going to school, constantly pestering his mother and eventually coming up with the idea of bribing the Professora into allowing him to join the class, even though he wasn't actually entitled to do so. This was because Vinha lay just over the county boundary and therefore outside Paiágua's catchment area. Officially, he should have gone to Sarnadas, but that was nearly five miles away, too far for a seven-year-old to walk each day. It was for this reason that children from Vinha, whose parents were anyway happier to have them working in the fields as soon as possible, had never bothered to go to school. A present of eggs and a home-made cake, baked specially by Mrs Pires, plus the initiative and enthusiasm that Lino showed in going along in person to plead his case, helped to convince the kindly Professora that this bright young lad deserved to be given the chance to get the education he so desperately wanted. Even at the tender age of seven, he had already realised that this could be his passport out of Vinha and to a brighter future.

Being an outsider, Lino was given a rough time by the local Paiágua boys, who would lie in wait for him each morning as he walked out of the forest, across the valley and up into the village on his way to school. There would be scuffles during which the prime target for the bullies would be Lino's hair, always neatly combed and parted even in those days. They would take great delight in messing it up. The same thing would happen after school, but Lino, undaunted, would wait until he got to the safety of the other side of the valley on his way home before turning to shout insults back at his tormentors. The next day, the same thing would start all over again. Lino happened to have an aunt living in Paiágua and, feeling sorry for him, Augusta would often run to the aunt's house, crying: "Come quickly! Come quickly! Lino is being beaten up again!"

However, it was to be a few years before Augusta began to take her young

Childhood sweethearts – they've spent a lifetime together.

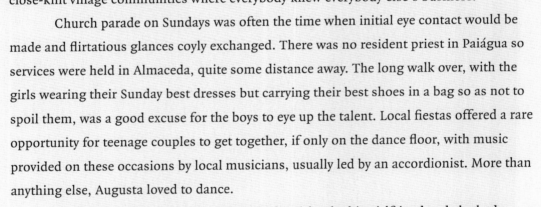

*More than anything, Augusta loved to dance to the sound
of music provided by local village musicians, usually led
by an accordionist.*

admirer's interest in her seriously and even then
their relationship remained very chaste. The
traditional rules of courtship in rural Portugal
in those days had to be strictly adhered to,
and woe betide any couple that dared to ignore them.
Not that there was the much opportunity for any hanky-panky in those
close-knit village communities where everybody knew everybody else's business.

Church parade on Sundays was often the time when initial eye contact would be
made and flirtatious glances coyly exchanged. There was no resident priest in Paiágua so
services were held in Almaceda, quite some distance away. The long walk over, with the
girls wearing their Sunday best dresses but carrying their best shoes in a bag so as not to
spoil them, was a good excuse for the boys to eye up the talent. Local fiestas offered a rare
opportunity for teenage couples to get together, if only on the dance floor, with music
provided on these occasions by local musicians, usually led by an accordionist. More than
anything else, Augusta loved to dance.

Once a young man had formally asked a girl to be his girlfriend and she had
agreed, he would then be allowed to visit her at her home, but would not be permitted to
enter the house. The two of them would simply chat across the threshold, as it were. When
the girl's parents eventually admitted her suitor to the house, it was a sign that things were
getting serious. People didn't so much 'go out' together as 'go in'.

Augusta was fifteen when Lino started writing to her again, once more asking her
to become his girlfriend. The letters were meant to be a secret at that stage, but when

Augusta's younger sister, Maria Santos, found out about them she couldn't resist the temptation to let the cat out of the bag. Mischievously, she revealed all to her parents, her triumphant giggles cut short as she was chased out of the house with threats of dire retribution from an angry, embarrassed and tearful Augusta.

By now, she had fallen for Lino's special charm. Not only was he a good-looking young man with a ready smile and an open, friendly manner; he also had boundless ambition and self-belief, combined with a wonderfully enthusiastic and positive outlook that was infectious, sweeping her along and helping her to overcome her own natural shyness and lack of self-confidence.

Her parents, meanwhile, were divided over whether he would make a suitable son-in-law. Her mother worried about the fact that he came from a much poorer family, believing that her daughter was in danger of marrying beneath her and that she could actually do much better for herself. Her father, on the other hand, had recognised straightaway that Lino was a hard worker and a fighter, with a driving determination to better himself. Mr Marques liked him. "With this man, Augusta will never starve," he promised his wife.

And so it was that after a few months Lino was invited into the house. He would go there for an hour or so each Thursday and Sunday evening and after sitting down and making polite conversation with the family for a while, he and Augusta would be allowed to retire to another room on their own. Even then, no physical contact of any kind was permitted. There was certainly no billing and cooing and necking was absolutely out of the question – they couldn't so much as hold hands. Instead, they would sit on opposite sides

Exquisite.
An example of Augusta's crochet work

of a table, chatting away and planning their future while Augusta got on with her spinning. If they ever met outside the house, her cousin, Maria da Graca, would usually be sent along as a chaperone, although Augusta admits with a smile that they could sometimes give the slip. "And Lino was very naughty!" she giggles.

Things carried on like this for the next six years, apart from an eighteen-month period when Lino was away doing his National Service. On his return to Vinha, he soon found himself slipping back into the same old routine – seasonal work on big estates around Castelo Branco during the grape and olive harvests, occasional labouring jobs on local road-building projects and various little enterprises on the side such as charcoal burning. At the same time, he was also expected to help his father out on the family's meagre few acres. Increasingly frustrated by the limitations of this existence, he was constantly looking for a way out.

Although Augusta loved the security of the village and family life and knew that she would miss both terribly if she left, she was as desperate as Lino to escape from the drudgery and the monotony of the dead-end routine that went with it. For a bright, intelligent and talented young woman, the thought of spending the rest of her life out in the fields in all weathers, in between confinements and the demands of raising a family,

Maria da Graca (Augusta's Cousin):

....

'Augusta and I had some wonderful times together. Just looking back and remembering it all makes me feel very emotional. We were so close — not just cousins but best friends, too, even though I was much younger.

"We both loved to dance. At fiesta time we would spend all night dancing. We would help organise the parties, decorate the street, prepare the meals and make sure we made really nice party clothes. One fiesta day to celebrate Sao Joao (St John), the patron saint of Paiágua, Augusta worked so hard that she fell asleep and didn't wake up until long after the party was over! During Quaresma (Lent) it was forbidden to dance, so we went to Augusta's house to dance in secret while I played the mouth organ, If our mothers had found out we had been dancing during Lent we would have been in big trouble.

When Augusta and Lino were courting, Augusta would ask me to make sure I stayed with them because Lino was so naughty. I would dutifully stay playing nearby, but Lino would eventually ask me to go fetch something. So I wasn't there all the time — and I think Augusta secretly liked that.'

....

held no appeal whatsoever. The main subject of conversation during those twice-weekly 'dates' with Lino in her back room would always be the same – the need to seek a better future for themselves away from Vinha and Paiágua.

In Salazar's Portugal, however, that was easier said than done – especially when you were trapped in the back-of-beyond. The country was poor, large towns relatively few and far between and communications generally very sketchy. With more and more people wanting to move into the towns and cities in search of work in the post-war years, jobs in these places were at a premium. In most cases, the only way to find one was through family connections – and, unfortunately, Lino had blown his only chance in that respect a few years earlier.

He had been only thirteen when his Godfather, Joseph Barata, managed to arrange a menial kitchen job for him in a small café in Castelo Branco that was owned by a friend of his. His duties involved mostly washing up and other chores, but he had stuck to it well and after a year was able to move on to a much better restaurant just off the town square. His job here was to walk round, dressed in a smart uniform, selling cigars, cigarettes and matches from a tray.

The owner of the restaurant was a wealthy Catholic priest who kindly provided Lino with free accommodation in the servants' quarters of his own large house, where the staff included five young maidservants. At some point, this proved too much of a temptation for Lino who was caught 'in flagrante' with one of the girls. Not surprisingly, in the circumstances, he was sent home in disgrace, although the priest, who had taken a liking to him, did say that he could have his job back in six months' time, once he had

"He's a fighter — with this man our daughter will never starve," said Augusta's father.
Lino during his National Service days and (top) in the uniform he wore for his first boyhood job,
selling cigars in a restaurant in Castelo Branco.

The boy most likely to succeed – Lino (fifth from left) at school:

❜ For me, it truly was love at first sight when I saw Augusta. I meant what I said in that
little note I left in her school desk – she definitely was the prettiest girl in the village.
And she was also very sweet-natured. That's why I made sure I was sitting next to her
in the classroom and why the Paiágua boys gave me such a hard time – they wanted
to keep her for themselves! And although my eye may have wandered a bit over the next
few years, she was the only one I was ever really interested in. I would never have
waited so long to marry her if I hadn't been worried about getting a good job first.
As it was, I was lucky not to lose her in the end. I had to move quickly. She's right in a
way when she jokes that I had to get married! But it was the best thing I ever did. ❜

cooled down a bit. Sadly, the priest then died before the six months was up and so the job was lost for ever.

The reputation that Lino had acquired as a result of this escapade was another reason why Augusta's mother was against the idea of her daughter getting too closely involved with him. Even Augusta's friends had warned her off. Lino, however, had managed to convince her that his bad boy image was undeserved. He explained that it had been a momentary lapse, that he had simply taken advantage of a situation that any red-blooded young man would have found impossible to resist and promised that he was a reformed character.

Augusta didn't need much persuading. She had had already decided that Lino was the one for her and was keen to get married as soon as possible. Lino, however, insisted that he must first get a decent job with prospects, otherwise he feared that they would never get away and would end up as peasant farmers, just like their parents. The trouble was that he had already tried everything he could think of, but the opportunities just weren't there. After completing his National Service he had thought about signing on as a regular soldier, but too many other people had got the same idea and there was a long waiting list; he had applied to join the police force but had failed the exam; he even considered becoming an illegal emigrant. Emigration was barred by the Salazar regime unless you could prove that you had a job to go to, but Lino had heard about a Roman Catholic father who was said to be smuggling men out of the country disguised as priests. However, he decided that this was too risky.

As time dragged on, Augusta began to despair. She even began to suspect that maybe Lino didn't really want to marry her after all. So, when a man from Lisbon happened to spot her while visiting friends in Paiágua and then started writing to her, she wrote back, partly to make Lino jealous but also because she was beginning to think that if all else failed, this might be her one chance to get away. Encouraged by this, her distant admirer then made a point of returning to Paiágua for a fiesta, but Augusta, seeing him for the first time, decided she didn't like him at all. He was, she told her family, "ugly and boring".

Lino, meanwhile, was also getting desperate and embarked on a madcap scheme that nearly cost him dear. Living not far away in the neighbouring village of Almaceda was a stunningly attractive girl who had caught the eye of just about every eligible male for miles around. However, it wasn't her looks that interested Lino so much as his discovery that she had relatives in Canada. He decided that he would quietly pretend to show interest in this girl just long enough to get in with her family well enough to be able to use their connections to fix himself up with a job in Canada. At that point he would find some excuse to end the relationship before things went too far. He and Augusta would then get married and go off to Canada together.

He somehow managed to convince himself that this devious plan might work. But, of course, it ended in tears as soon as Augusta found out that he was apparently two-timing her – and that didn't take very long! After he had mysteriously failed to put in an appearance at a local village fiesta where she had been expecting to meet up with him, word soon reached her that on that very same evening he had been spotted paying court to the girl in Almaceda.

Wedding day, April 1957. The happy couple (top) and (bottom) flanked by their godparents. On the left, Lino's godparents, Jose and Maria Barata, and on the right Augusta's uncle and godfather, Augusto, and her elder sister, Maria Marques.

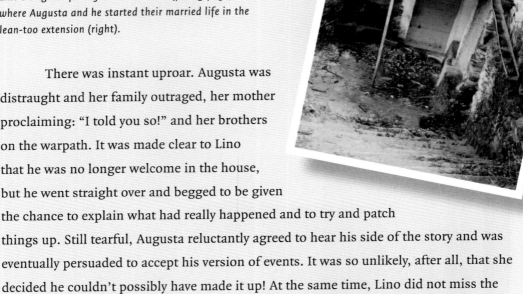

Lino's original family home in Vinha (facing page) where Augusta and he started their married life in the lean-too extension (right).

There was instant uproar. Augusta was distraught and her family outraged, her mother proclaiming: "I told you so!" and her brothers on the warpath. It was made clear to Lino that he was no longer welcome in the house, but he went straight over and begged to be given the chance to explain what had really happened and to try and patch things up. Still tearful, Augusta reluctantly agreed to hear his side of the story and was eventually persuaded to accept his version of events. It was so unlikely, after all, that she decided he couldn't possibly have made it up! At the same time, Lino did not miss the opportunity to remind her about the gentleman from Lisbon!

Her family, however, remained understandably sceptical and Lino realised that there was only one way to convince them that his intentions were wholly honourable. Waiting only to tell his parents what he was planning to do, he returned a few days later and made a formal proposal of marriage. It had always been his intention to wait until he had found the job he wanted, but his only concern now was to make sure he didn't lose the girl he had fallen in love with the moment he first saw her. As Augusta always takes great delight in telling everybody, with a nudge and a wink: "He had to get married, you know – but not for the usual reason!"

The wedding took place in the village chapel of Senhora Das Dores in April 1957. The whole village turned out to wish the couple well and friends and relatives came from all over the surrounding area to join the festivities. Augusta looked stunning in the long white wedding dress that she had made herself, with help from her older sister, Delfina. Lino was his usual immaculate self for the most part – although not quite from head to toe! The day before the ceremony he had slipped and cut his foot quite badly while fishing in the local river, so he had to wear carpet slippers instead of shoes except for when he limped up the aisle. The celebrations lasted for two whole days, with much eating and drinking, but there was no honeymoon for the happy couple. Instead, they spent their wedding night on a straw mattress in a corner of the dusty barn that was normally used to store animal feed, but which had been cleared out to serve as the venue for the reception. Impatient for their first kiss, the newlyweds had to wait for the last guest to leave before they could get to bed.

The next day they moved into the Pires family home in Vinha, where Lino had added a one-room lean-to extension to the back of what was little more than a hovel. And on the Monday morning he went off to work as a labourer for Augusta's uncle. His job there was to collect resin from pine trees, a particularly mind-numbing task that involved trudging ten miles a day from one stand of trees to the next to tap the resin. As he toiled through the heat of the day, returning each evening at dusk to the shack-like room that Augusta had done her best to turn into a home, Lino became even more determined than ever to get away.

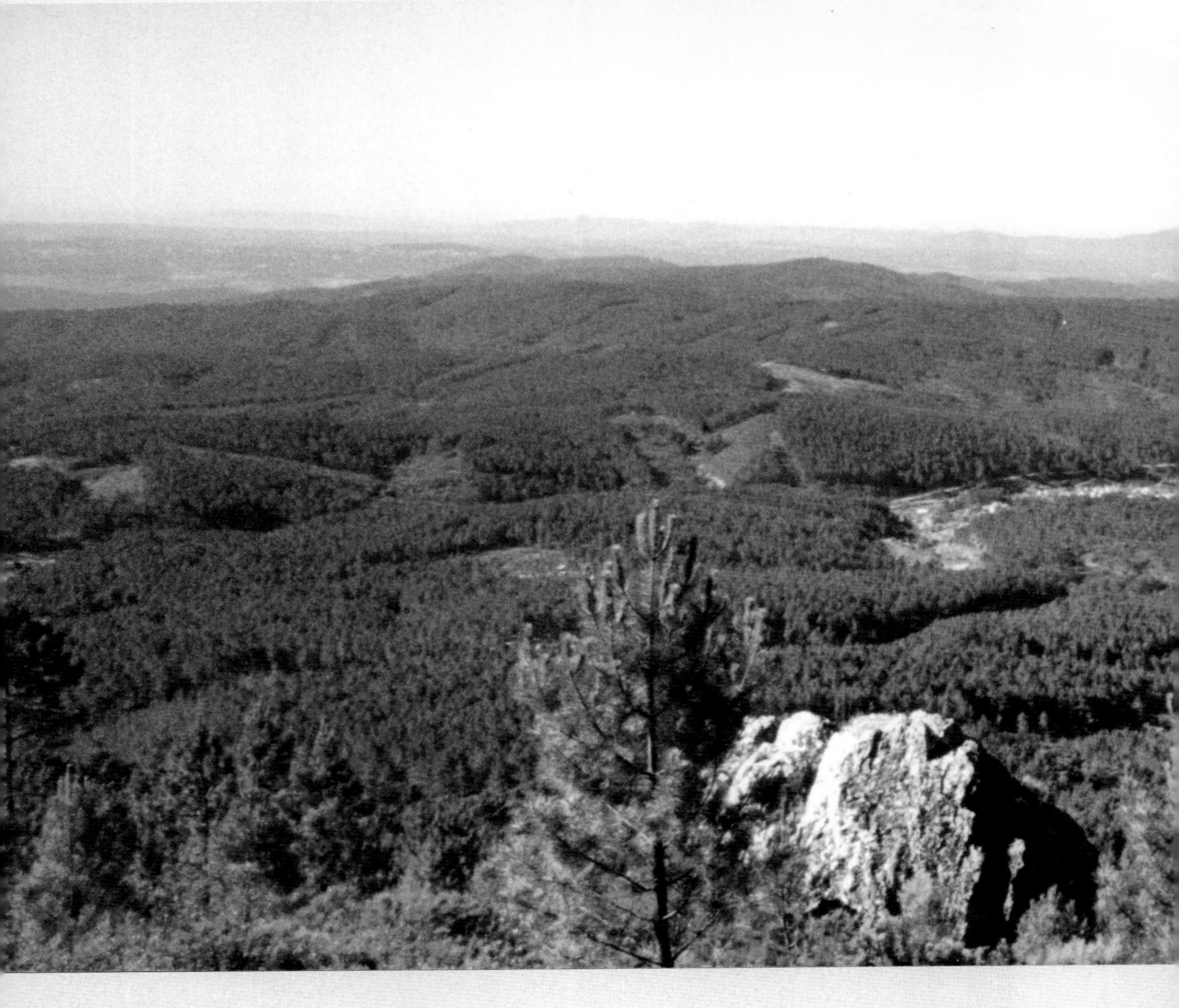

The view looking across to Paiágua from the hillside olive grove owned by Augusta's family.

Fried Marrows and Aubergines

We loved to cook this in the summer when we had plenty of vegetables, using the same principle as French toast.

> marrow
> aubergines
> flour
> beaten egg
> salt and pepper
> olive oil

Remove the skin from the marrow and scoop out the seeds. Slice the marrow and aubergines and sprinkle the aubergines with a little salt to remove some of the moisture and bitterness.

Season and dip into the beaten egg, dust in flour and fry in the olive oil.

Canja
CHICKEN AND RICE SOUP

We never killed young chickens to roast in Paiágua. Chickens were kept for their eggs. When they became old and stopped laying, they were too tough to do anything with other than make a chicken soup called Canja to which we added little noodles or rice. It is so nutritious that we gave this soup to people who were unwell, or to women who had just had a baby. My mother once gave it to our cow who was ill – and she recovered! We all swore it had been the soup.

SERVES 4–6

1 stewing chicken (cut into pieces)

2 onions

1 clove garlic

4 pints/2.2 litres water

7 oz/200g long grain rice, small pasta shapes or noodles

1 tablespoon chopped parsley

salt and freshly ground black pepper

Rinse the chicken pieces and season with salt and pepper. Place in a large stockpot or flameproof casserole, along with the onions, garlic and water. Bring to the boil and simmer for two hours, removing all the scum from the surface as it forms.

When the chicken is tender transfer it to a plate to cool. Remove the bones and shred the chicken. Return to the pot, add the rice or noodles and any further seasoning if required. Reduce heat to low, cover casserole and cook for another 30 minutes or until the rice or noodles are cooked. Stir in the parsley.

Arroz Doce
PORTUGUESE RICE PUDDING

This was a really popular dish in Portugal. My mother made the most wonderful rice pudding and I still vividly remember her cooking it in the copper pot. Some of the rice would get stuck to the bottom of the pot and I always begged her to let me scrape it up. It was deliciously sticky and sweet.

It is the same recipe as we have in The Butcher's Arms today. I taught our first chef Simon, how to cook it and now it is one of the most requested desserts on the trolley.

SERVES 6–8

2 pints/1.2 litre of full fat milk	3 egg yolks
10½ oz/300g sugar	rind from one orange (use a vegetable peeler)
10½ oz/300g pudding rice	stick of cinnamon
1¾ pint/1 litre water	bay leaf
3½ fl oz/100ml cream	cinnamon powder (optional)
3½ oz/100g butter	pinch of salt

Bring the milk, orange rind, bay leaf, stick of cinnamon and the sugar to the boil. Put the pudding rice and water along with a pinch of salt, into a separate pan and bring to the boil. Boil for three minutes. Strain the rice and add it to the boiling milk. Reduce the heat and simmer slowly until the rice is very soft. Take off the heat, remove the bay leaf, cinnamon and orange skin. Add the butter, egg yolks and cream.

Pour into a serving dish and allow to cool and set. Serve with ground cinnamon on top.

Sintra's famed Palacio da Pena.

Part Three

Sintra

WITHIN WEEKS OF GETTING MARRIED,
AUGUSTA FOUND HERSELF SEPARATED FROM
HER HUSBAND.

Although tearful for the first few days after Lino left, she knew in her heart that it was for the best. The reason for his sudden departure was that he had at last managed to land the sort of job that offered the prospect of an eventual lifeline out of Vinha for the two of them. The only problem, in the short term, was that it meant him being away on his own for the first few months.

It was Augusta's sister-in-law, Esmerelda, who had eventually come up trumps, using her influence to find a lowly position for Lino at the five-star Palacio de Seteais hotel, 120 miles away in Sintra, just outside Lisbon. Married to Augusta's elder brother, Joseph, Esmerelda was the niece of one of the partners who owned both the Seteais and the Tivoli Hotel in Lisbon. She herself was already working at the Seteais as the housekeeper in charge of all the bedrooms and, after pulling a few strings, she had succeeded in fixing Lino up with a menial job as a male chambermaid. It wasn't much, but it was a start and Lino gratefully seized the opportunity with both hands.

His decision to go on ahead by himself, leaving Augusta behind, was prompted by the fact that just before he got the job he had bought a new house for his parents in Vinha – despite the extension, the place they were in just wasn't big enough with him and Augusta living there as well – and for a while most of his wages would have to go towards paying off the small mortgage he had arranged. But after six months he had cleared the debt and felt sufficiently settled and financially secure to be able to send for Augusta to join him.

Shy by nature and always lacking in self-confidence, Augusta viewed the move with alarm. Although now twenty-three years of age, she had still never been further from home than Castelo Branco and found even that a bit unnerving. She had never forgotten how the local kids had poked fun at her for being an ignorant peasant when she had been taken there for the first time as a young teenager and had been unable to hide her amazement at seeing electric lights for the first time. That humiliating experience had made a deep impression on her. Now, having lived her entire life amid the security of a tightly-knit village community in which she had known almost every single inhabitant for as long as she could remember, she was about to be pitched into the completely alien environment of a fashionable European resort on the fringes of Portugal's capital city, a place where she would know virtually nobody. It was a truly frightening prospect for a timid country girl and there were plenty more tears as she boarded the train at Castelo Branco and waved her parents goodbye. She was accompanied on the journey by her twelve-year-old nephew, Jose, who had also been found a job at the Seteais – as a bellboy.

The first few weeks in Sintra were every bit as difficult and bewildering as she had feared. Lino had rented a single room for them to live in just off the main square in Sintra and had also arranged a job for Augusta as a cleaner in a small bar restaurant called *Adega Das Caves* that was owned by their landlord. The work there turned out to be almost as hard as labouring in the fields back home in Paiágua, her day starting at four o'clock in the

The Palacio de Seteais, one of the world's great hotels.

The clifftop village of Azenhas do Mar,
near Sintra (main picture) and (below) Augusta and Lino and
friends enjoying a day off on the beach at Praia Maças.

morning when she would have to get up to scrub the floors and do the washing-up before walking to market with the owner to help him with the food shopping for the restaurant, struggling back laden down with heavy bags.

Lino, meanwhile, was working overtime at the Seteais, volunteering to help out wherever he was needed in the hotel once his official room cleaning duties had been completed, simply in order to find out at first hand how everything was done in the various departments. Desperately keen to advance himself, he missed no opportunity to acquire new skills and to gain valuable experience, even going so far as to pay for his own waiter's uniform just so that he could gain access to the dining room and learn how to serve teas and lay up tables for dinner.

Both he and Augusta were so busy and working such long hours at this time that they hardly saw each other during the day, Augusta rising well before dawn to start her cleaning duties at the bar and Lino often coming back quite late in the evening after his extra volunteer stints at the Seteais. They would occasionally meet during lunch breaks to go for a brief walk around Sintra's picturesque streets and gardens or to enjoy a cup of coffee at one of the cafes in the square. And sometimes, at weekends, they would take a picnic down to the beach, travelling on the tram that ran the four miles from Sintra down to Praia Maças and Praia Grande, the latter regarded as one of the finest beaches in the whole of Portugal. Little could they have ever imagined as they sat there on the sand, eating their sandwiches, that they would one day own a villa in a prime spot overlooking that very beach.

Their conversations on these occasions would often focus on Lino's increasingly ambitious plans for the future, Augusta listening patiently as he outlined his latest schemes, never really daring to share his belief that these dreams would eventually come true. Even at this early stage, Lino was already showing signs of a budding entrepreneurial streak, having become convinced that the only way to do really well for yourself was to have your own business.

He and Augusta had only been in Sintra together for about six months when he conceived the idea of taking on the tenancy of a small coffee bar in one of the narrow streets just off the square. Lino reckoned it was in the perfect location, with bags of potential for development, but, unfortunately, he didn't have the £100 needed to secure the lease. Undeterred, he tried to talk Augusta's other brother, Francisco, into joining him in the venture.

Francisco was married to the sister of Joseph's wife, Esmerelda – an unusual instance of two brothers having married two sisters – and, as a result, both he and Joseph had been fixed up with top jobs at the Seteais by the girls' uncle, who part-owned the place. Lino knew that Francisco had quite a bit of money saved up, so he went to him with a proposition. If Francisco would put up the money for the lease, his wife and Augusta could work full-time in the café and he and Lino would help out on their days off. Then, as soon as the venture started making a profit, Francisco could take his £100 off the top, plus interest, after which he and Lino would own the business 50/50. Francisco was initially very keen, but then changed his mind at the very last moment so that the whole deal fell through, much to Lino's frustration.

To this day, he still frets over the missed opportunity, pointing out that many

José Peres (Augusta's nephew):

⸱⸱⸱

❛ Like Augusta, I grew up in Paiágua and my first memory of her was one fiesta day
when I was very small and I distinctly remember seeing her with her three sisters – all
dressed exactly the same and looking very beautiful.

When I was 12 years old, Lino fixed me up with a job as a bellboy at the Seteais Hotel,
where he was already working. It was decided that Augusta and I would travel
up together. It was a big adventure for us because neither of us had travelled so
far in our lives and we had never been on a train.

I was frightened, being so young, but I think Augusta who was much older,
was even more frightened than me because she worried that we wouldn't be able to find
Lino at the station when we arrived. And when the train went through a tunnel,
we were both so scared.

We didn't know that trains could go through mountains! Augusta and Lino became
a big part of my life and were my surrogate parents for many years. When I was 18,
I went to England to join Lino at The Three Horseshoes in Rugby and then for
seven years I worked as his head waiter at The Butcher's Arms. I loved my time
there. The atmosphere was terrific and the customers were great.

But it was Augusta that helped make my time in England so special. She is a true lady,
a fine woman who is kind to everybody and totally devoted to her family.
And we always had such fun together. She just loves to make people laugh. ❜

⸱⸱⸱

others who started similar businesses in Portugal at around the same time went on to become 'multi-multi-millionaires', as he puts it. He has to be reminded that he hasn't done so badly himself – and Sintra's loss has turned out to be Warwickshire's gain. Augusta was never that bothered about missing out on the café. "I have always been fatalistic about these things," she says. "My feeling at the time was that if it happened, it happened – if not, then it was obviously not meant to be. And, looking back, if we had ended up with the café we would never have had *The Butcher's Arms* and would not have met so many wonderful people."

While Augusta found difficulty in adjusting to her new and very different lifestyle in Sintra, Lino seemed to be instantly in his element amid the glitz and glamour of the Seteais. In the days before the advent of jet aircraft led to the birth of the so-called 'international jet set', it was on luxury ocean liners that the rich and famous cruised the world. Lisbon was a key port of call, Sintra a renowned resort and the Seteais the fashionable place to stay. The regular VIP guest list there included the cream of European royalty and aristocracy, show business celebrities, business tycoons and all manner of VIPs – from the young Princess Margaret to General Franco and from Agatha Christie to David Niven.

Lino would often return home to Augusta in their cramped little room in the evenings with gossip about the celebrities who had been seen arriving in great limousines and whom he then glimpsed in the cocktail bar or the dining room. Lino himself served David Niven on several occasions during the great star's honeymoon stay there with his wife, Hjordis. So, too, did Augusta's little nephew, José, already becoming a hit with the guests in his new job as a bellboy. José who was to become head waiter at *The Butcher's Arms* many years later, was too small to heft the Nivens' heavy suitcases and left them to do it themselves while he trotted along in front of them with the room key. Despite this, the couple were so amused by him that they singled him out for a special tip when they left at the end of their stay.

Augusta, meanwhile, had quit her job at the Adega Das Caves in anticipation of working in Lino's planned café and when that fell through she found herself at a loose end. At this point, Fate then intervened when a British couple, Peter and Margaret Tahany, came to the Seteais on holiday with their two children. Their arrival was destined to be the single event that would decide Augusta and Lino's future, changing the whole direction of their lives fundamentally and forever.

A tall and impressive-looking man, a former rugby blue from Oxford University who went on to become a top international referee, Peter Tahany ran a highly successful engineering business in the Midlands. He and his wife had come to Portugal with their two young sons, Paul and Justin, and, being pregnant with their third child, Mrs Tahany had asked the manager whether it might be possible to find someone to look after the younger of the two boys, three-year-old Justin, so that she could have some time to herself. The manager then approached Lino and asked him if Augusta might be prepared to take on the job.

Augusta wasn't keen at first, pointing out that she couldn't speak a word of English. However, the manager assured her that this wouldn't really matter since Justin, being only three, would not need to be spoken to that much and so she eventually agreed. Her natural warmth and gentle maternal nature then ensured that she did a marvellous job, entertaining the boys in the hotel gardens or taking them down to the beach to play in the sand. The Tahanys were so impressed that at the end of their stay they asked if she would

Augusta outside the bar/restaurant in Sintra where she worked.

António Reis – 'Tony' (An old friend from Augusta's Sintra days):

....

❛ I was working as a chauffeur and taxi driver at the Seteais Hotel when Lino and Augusta were there, so I got to know them very well. I felt very proud that Lino trusted me to drive them down to the port to board the ship that was to take them to their new life in England. I still remember that day in 1960 very well. I picked them up from their flat in Sintra and during the half-hour journey to the harbour Augusta said very little. She was very apprehensive and nervous and especially worried because she couldn't speak English.

Now, nearly 40 years later, I still drive Lino and Augusta around when they come back to Portugal – as well as all their friends that come out to visit. And even though we are far apart we still keep in touch. Lino rings me to give me their news, so I am always able to keep up with what is happening in

their life. Following their success over the years has been a great pleasure. Like all their friends and their family in Portugal, I'm very proud of them and what they have achieved. Their way of life may have changed, but they are still the same kind, hard working people they always were. ❜

....

consider going to live with them at their home in England as a full-time nanny and cook once the new baby arrived. When it was then explained that she had a husband – "You know Lino, he works in the bedrooms" – they immediately invited him to go as well, offering him a job as a general handyman.

This gave both Augusta and Lino considerable pause for thought. Apart from those odd moments of desperation when Lino had vaguely considered emigration as a last resort in his efforts to find a future for himself away from Vinha, neither of them had ever thought seriously about going abroad and leaving their families and friends behind.

For Augusta, especially, the whole idea was terrifying. She had found it difficult enough moving from Paiágua to Sintra; now, just as she was beginning to get used to that situation, she was being asked to uproot herself again and disappear to what seemed to her like the other side of the world. There were a number of very tearful and anxious discussions. Even Lino, although he was tempted by thoughts of the money they would earn and the tales he had heard of 'expatriates' who had gone abroad and done very well for themselves, was not entirely sure that it was the right thing to do. At the same time, he had been frustrated by the collapse of the coffee shop venture. And he figured that even if things didn't work out in England, they could always come back and, with the money they would be able to save by living in with the Tahanys, they would then have the wherewithal to set up in business on their own in Portugal. Augusta remained tearful and far from convinced, but, as has been the case throughout their long relationship, she put her trust in Lino and left him to make the big decision.

In the end, he came to the conclusion that they had nothing much to lose by going.

Even then, it wasn't straightforward. Normally, it could take anything up to three years
to go through the lengthy process of getting a passport and completing all the other
formalities involved in getting clearance to move abroad from Portugal under the Salazar
regime. And yet the Tahanys needed them within a matter of weeks, as soon as the new
baby was born. Once again, Lino used his charm to find a short cut.

As with everything in Portugal in those days, what you needed in such a situation
was a good contact with influence. Among the regular guests at the Seteais was a very
grand lady named Senhora Fernanda Bandiera de Lima, whose husband just happened to
be the Minister in charge of the Emigration Office. She would often be in her suite while
Lino was making up the bed and, in his characteristic friendly fashion, he would chat away
to her while he worked, even though there was a strict rule forbidding staff from speaking
to guests unless spoken to, on pain of instant dismissal. The Senhora, however, seemed to
enjoy their conversations and had obviously warmed to Lino, so much so that he felt
emboldened to explain the situation he was in and to ask whether there was any way in
which she might be able to use her influence to help speed things up. Without hesitation,
she sat down there and then and wrote out a letter which, when he presented it at the
Emigration Office, resulted in him acquiring passports for himself and Augusta and all
the other necessary documentation within two days!

As the day of their departure rapidly approached, Augusta became increasingly
apprehensive about the huge step they were taking. Neither her parents nor Lino's could
contemplate journeying all the way to Lisbon to see them off, so the couple returned to
Vinha and Paiágua to say their final farewells to the families, not knowing how long it

would be before they would see them or even speak to them again. As things turned out, it was to be four years.

Back in Sintra, Augusta carefully packed their very few worldly belongings into two cheap suitcases and then António Reis, the hotel chauffeur, drove them down to the quayside and they boarded the ship. A few friends came down to wave them off and, after settling into their cabin for the three-day voyage, they went back up on deck to watch as she ship left harbour. Augusta was sick with nerves. "Imagine how I felt," she says. "Going to Lisbon had been bad enough. Now this! For me, going to England seemed like going to the end of the world. I thought that I would never be going back and that I would never see my parents again." She and Lino stood at the rail until the Portuguese coastline finally slipped out of sight beyond the horizon and as they turned away to go below Augusta was in floods of tears, fearful of what the future might hold.

Grilled Sardines

Portugal is famous for its sardines. We didn't eat them in Paiágua because we were too far from the sea, but I never forget tasting them for the first time in Sintra after we were married. I love to grill them very plainly on the barbecue, simply sprinkled with salt and pepper, and then eat them with salad and roasted peppers. However, if you want to add a bit of extra flavour you can season them with rosemary, garlic and olive oil.

SERVES 4

1½ lbs/700g fresh sardines

2 sprigs of fresh rosemary

2 cloves of garlic, peeled and crushed

3 tablespoons of olive oil

salt and pepper

Preheat the grill. Leave the heads on the sardines but slit along the belly and clean under cold running water.

Pat dry with kitchen paper. Place on the grill pan. Brush the sardines with oil and sprinkle with half the rosemary leaves. Grill for 4–5 minutes until just beginning to turn brown. Turn the sardines and brush with more oil and sprinkle with the rest of the rosemary leaves. Grill for a further 4–5 minutes. Serve immediately.

Caldeirada de Peixe
FISH STEW

This is a real fisherman's stew, the Portuguese version of the French bouillabaisse but the spices and herbs in this dish give it a real Portuguese flavour. It is a meal in itself and I would cook this when we lived in Sintra where I would buy the fish from the little market in Praia Grande. The ingredients were always dependent on what the boats brought in but it is important to use fish with a firm flesh.

In later years, when we lived in Priors Hardwick I would buy the fish from a wonderful fishmonger in Leamington Spa. I was always careful to choose the best fish. Even though this is a fish stew, do not be tempted to use offcuts.

SERVES 4

1 lb/450g monkfish tail
½ lb/225g swordfish or tuna
¾ lb/350g white fish such as cod
   or haddock
½ lb/225g large raw prawns
12 clams
12 mussels
3 garlic cloves, chopped
3 tablespoons olive oil
1 large green pepper
2 onions, roughly chopped
6 medium potatoes, peeled and
   cut in large chunks
2 x 14 oz cans chopped tomatoes or
   fresh, skinned tomatoes

1 bay leaf
3 teaspoons piri piri sauce
1 glass dry white wine
1 cup of water
chopped fresh coriander
salt and pepper to taste

Clean the fish and cut into 2 inch pieces. Place them in a bowl with the garlic, 2 tablespoons olive oil and a light seasoning of salt and pepper. Let it marinate for 15 to 20 minutes.

Cut the pepper into thin strips. In a large saucepan or oven-to-table casserole pot, heat the remaining oil and stir in the pepper strips and onions. Add the potatoes and sprinkle with a little salt. Add the chopped tomatoes, bay leaf, piri piri sauce and one cup of water. Cover and bring to simmering point. Cook for 20 minutes.

If using clams place them around the perimeter of the pan and place the pieces of monkfish and swordfish in the centre. Add the mussels and prawns. Put the cod or haddock on top, pour the wine over the fish and sprinkle with pepper. Cook for 10 more minutes until the fish is cooked through and the clams and mussels are open. Discard any that don't open.

Ladle the stew into large bowls and sprinkle with the chopped coriander. Serve with crusty bread.

The stove on which Augusta did all the cooking when she and Lino began married life in Sintra.

Pasteis de Nata
PORTUGUESE CUSTARD TARTS

These rich egg custard tarts are famous in Portugal. They were first made at the Antiga Confeitaria de Belem, in Lisbon. When friends come to stay with us in Portugal we often take them to the shop to buy some of these wonderfully more-ish tarts.

MAKES 12 TARTLETS

1 packet of frozen puff pastry, thawed

8oz/225g caster sugar

9 fl oz/250ml milk

2 tablespoons cornflour

½ teaspoon vanilla extract

6 egg yolks

cinnamon

nutmeg

Preheat the oven to 200 C. Lightly grease a muffin or tartlet tray. Roll out the puff pasty, sprinkle with nutmeg, cinnamon and a little sugar. Fold up the pastry and roll out again. Cut into 12 rounds and line the cups, pricking the base of each case.

In a saucepan combine the milk, cornflour, sugar and vanilla. Cook, stirring constantly, until the mixture thickens. Place the egg yolks in a bowl, slowly whisk half of the warm milk mixture into the egg yolks. Gradually add the egg yolk mixture back into the remaining milk mixture, whisking all the time. Cook, stirring, for five minutes or until thickened.

Fill the pastry-lined muffin cases with the mixture and bake for 20 minutes or until the crust is golden brown and the filling is lightly browned on top.

To serve, sprinkle with a little icing sugar and ground cinnamon.

When in Lisbon, a visit to the Antiga Confeitaria de Belem
is a must for anyone with a sweet tooth.

Augusta on the terrace steps at Claybrooke Grange,
with Peter Tahany in his pram in the background.

Part Four

Claybrooke

The England that Augusta and Lino arrived in one damp, grey autumn morning in 1960 was a very different place from what it is today.

It is easy to forget just how much things have changed over the years since then. The 'Swinging Sixties' had yet to revolutionise the social scene and the old order was still in place to such an extent that a learned barrister could stand up in court during the Lady Chatterley trial and seriously question whether people would want their "wives or servants" to read such a book. Television's 'That Was The Week That Was' and the satire boom had not yet undermined the culture of deference that had sustained the Establishment and kept everybody else in their place. Spreading affluence had only just begun to break down the old class barriers and the average wage was well under £10-a-week. There were relatively few cars on the road and the country's first motorway, the M1, had only recently been opened as far as Birmingham. Only the well-to-do went out to eat on a regular basis, except, perhaps, to a Lyons Cornerhouse. There were no supermarkets, so High Streets were still full of butchers, bakers, greengrocers and fishmongers. And it would be a while before the Clean Air Act would gradually put an end to the smogs that regularly choked our winter cities.

Disembarking at Tilbury, Augusta and Lino gazed about them in wonder as they walked down the gangway from the ship that had brought them over from Portugal. Clutching their suitcases, they scanned the quayside below for a sign of the driver that they had been told by the Tahanys would be waiting there to pick them up. It wasn't until they came through customs that they eventually spotted him, holding up a board with the word PIRES written on it in large capitals.

Since neither of them could speak any English and the driver certainly knew no Portuguese, there was no conversation during the three-hour journey up to Leicestershire. Sitting in the back, their noses pressed to the windows on either side as they were driven through London and onto the M1, Augusta and Lino remained mostly silent, hardly even speaking to each other, except to draw attention to some landmark or other point of interest. Augusta had not known quite what to expect, but, among her first impressions, she was immediately struck by how fresh and green the countryside was, while the towns seemed rather grey and drab.

Claybrooke Grange, Peter and Margaret Tahany's home, was right out in the country, about fifteen miles from Leicester. A large, rambling house, it stood in grounds of about ten acres that included gardens and paddocks. The new arrivals were given a warm welcome by Mr and Mrs Tahany and the two boys. However, language difficulties made communication rather awkward, with both sides having to resort to a great deal of mime and frequent references to the large English/Portuguese dictionary in which Mr Tahany had thoughtfully invested.

The first real misunderstanding came very early on. After showing Augusta and Lino to their rooms and allowing them time to unpack and get settled in, Mrs Tahany asked what

The new arrivals at the Grange were given a warm welcome by Mr and Mrs Tahany and their sons.

Peter Tahany (whose parents brought Augusta over to England in 1960):

....

' It was Augusta's outstanding maternal instincts that prompted my parents to employ her as

my nanny. That was what so impressed them when she helped to look after my older brothers

Paul and Justin during that holiday at the Seteais shortly before I was born.

I was still only two when she left Claybrooke Grange to go and work at The Three Horse

Shoes, so I don't remember anything about her at the time, but I am told that she used to

spoil me rotten. My mother had fairly traditional Victorian views about child rearing that

included putting me out on the terrace every afternoon to make sure I got plenty of fresh air.

The story goes that as soon as I heard the sound of my mother's car going down the drive

I would hang my hands out of the pram until they turned blue whereupon Augusta

would rush out and bring me inside!

I can quite believe the stories about spoiling because the whole family has kept in touch

with them over the years and now, whenever we see them, Augusta is exactly the

same with my two children, Cordelia and Jasper. She just has that natural maternal

instinct that is unqualified and timeless.

It's been wonderful to share vicariously in their success over the years and the fact that

I myself now have an interest in several restaurants in London may well be more than

a co-incidence. My appreciation of good food and fine wine must have been nurtured at

an early age through regular visits to The Butcher's Arms.

I am greatly flattered that Lino and Augusta should have named their own son after me. '

....

they would like to do for supper that evening and suggested that maybe a Spanish omelette would be a good idea. That would be perfect, replied Augusta, nodding enthusiastically. Having been shown where to find everything in the kitchen, she soon prepared the omelette, which she and Lino then ate. Some time later, Mrs Tahany popped her head around the kitchen door and, looking slightly puzzled, asked how the omelette was going.

"Oh, very good, thank you," replied the couple, Lino patting his stomach appreciatively and smacking his lips. "Very tasty!"

On hearing this, Margaret Tahany burst out laughing. She had actually been expecting Augusta to make supper for her and Mr Tahany, she explained. As Augusta was going to be cooking for the family as part of her duties, she had deliberately suggested a Spanish omelette as something simple and easy to start off with on her first day.

After that, Augusta decided that she and Lino would have to make a real effort to learn English. This was easier said than done when you were living out in the sticks, but they did eventually find a Portuguese-speaking teacher in Leicester who was prepared to give private lessons. At the same time, Mr Tahany very gamely tried to learn Portuguese. Even so, there were further comical misunderstandings from time to time.

The most hilarious example occurred when Mr Tahany came home from work one evening and, picking his words very carefully, announced that he had found his grandmother dead in his car. Augusta was understandably shocked until she realised that he had made the very easy mistake of confusing the word 'avo', meaning grandmother, with 'ave', meaning bird. What he was trying to tell her was that a bird had been hit by the car and had got stuck in the radiator grille.

Although she soon settled into the routine at the Grange, where she and Lino were treated very well indeed by the family, Augusta became very homesick once the excitement of coming to England and the novelty of her new life began to wear off. Paiágua might as well have been on the other side of the world. There were no telephones in the village in those days, so there was no way she could speak to her parents and her family back home. The only communication was by letter, and the post took ages to get there. Any mail would only be delivered as far as the post office in Almaceda, where it would be kept until somebody from Paiágua happened to drop in and was able to collect it.

Desperate for any sort of contact with home, Augusta and Lino bought a radio and Mr Tahany then helped them to rig up a special aerial in the hope of being able to pick up a Portuguese station. Unfortunately, this didn't work and in the end the only Portuguese language station they could find anywhere on the dial was a regular Voice of Moscow Communist propaganda broadcast that was beamed back to Portugal from Russia late at night, urging revolution against the Salazar regime. Augusta had no interest in politics, but she would tune in just to hear someone speaking Portuguese.

She and Lino were also provided with a television set in their living room next to the kitchen and they would watch it even though they couldn't understand what was being said, just because it was such a novelty. Television had only arrived in Portugal in 1957 and very few people had got sets by the time they left, so they had virtually never seen TV before arriving in England. Even here, you could only get a black and white picture – colour television didn't come in until 1967. Augusta actually managed to improve her English by first watching the news on television

Radio, television and a large English/Portuguese dictionary helped overcome language problems.

Peter Tahany Snr:

. . . .

❛ Augusta has such a sweet personality – that was certainly what made the
greatest impression on my wife and I when she looked after Justin and Paul at
the Seteais in Portugal. She was also particularly good with children, even
though she had none of her own at that time. We realised straightaway that
she would make a perfect nanny for Peter. And Lino was such a hard worker
that we were only too happy to have him as well.

Augusta, especially, used to get very homesick. I do well remember trying to rig
up this long-distance aerial so that she could pick up Portuguese programmes,
but I fear it didn't work very well.

When they left us, I had no difficulty fixing them up with jobs at The Three
Horse Shoes. Being a regular there, I knew the owners and the managers very
well indeed and had no hesitation in recommending Lino and Augusta to them.
And I'm not at all surprised that they have gone on to do so well for themselves.

Lino had such drive and ambition and Augusta was always 100% behind
him in everything. They made a great team. ❜

. . . .

and then trying to follow reports of the same items in the newspaper the next day.

Her favourite programme, however, was the comedy series *Bootsy and Snudge*. She still couldn't understand a word, but hotel porter Bootsy's uniform was exactly the same as the one Lino had worn at the Seteais and there was something about the way he would cough politely and hold his hand out behind his back for a tip that always had tears of laughter rolling down Augusta's face.

She was very happy looking after baby Peter and the two older Tahany boys, who were very polite and well-behaved, although not averse to taking advantage of her when the opportunity arose. When Mr Tahany overheard Justin calling his brother "a bastard", he came storming into the kitchen and gave him a severe ticking off, telling him: "Don't you ever let me hear you use that word in this house again!"

"But I asked Augusta if I could say it and she said yes," retorted Justin with an air of sweet innocence. This was quite true, but although he obviously knew perfectly well that it was a rude word, he was also smart enough to realise that Augusta wouldn't have a clue what it meant, allowing him to get away with using it and then blaming her if he was caught out. Ever since then it has been Augusta's favourite terms of abuse!

In addition to her nannying duties, Augusta also enjoyed cooking and soon spiced up the menu at the Grange. Plain stews and casseroles were livened up no end with the addition of various herbs and seasoning not normally used in traditional English home cooking at the time, while vegetables from the kitchen garden were served up in all sorts of imaginative ways instead of simply being boiled or steamed. She produced wonderfully tasty vegetable soups, made in the way that her mother had taught her. And the Tahanys' dinner guests, for whom she also cooked, all wanted to be given the recipe for her Portuguese rice pudding.

Lino, meanwhile, kept himself busy by doing the gardening as well as the housework. On their days off, the two of them would sometimes take the bus into Leicester, where they would spend an hour or two walking around the shops, buying sweets in Woolworth's and maybe stopping off somewhere for a coffee. In some ways, it was a lonely, isolated existence, but the Tahanys were very friendly and did their best to make them feel at home.

They stayed with the family for two years and might well have remained at the Grange much longer had it not been for a rather unexpected development. Little Peter Tahany, who had been born very shortly after they arrived, was slow to start talking, so much so that his worried parents eventually took him to see a specialist in an effort to find out what was holding him back. The specialist suggested that one possible reason might be that he was spending a lot of his time with Augusta and Lino who would always be speaking Portuguese to each other and that this might have confused him in some way. In the circumstances, his parents reluctantly came to the conclusion that it might indeed be better if he had an English nanny.

As it turned out, Peter's slow start clearly didn't cause any long-term problems because he went on to become a highly successful lawyer and corporate financier and also, as it happens, part owner of several top restaurants in London. And he revealed to Augusta and Lino years later that his own son had been equally slow to start talking, so that it was probably a simple genetic thing.

On their days off, the two of
them would sometimes take the
bus into Leicester.

Augusta with Peter Tahany (facing page) in the
grounds of Claybrooke Grange and (right) with
Peter and Justin.

Augusta had grown very fond of Peter
during the two years she was looking after him,
so much so that she named her own son after him.
"He was such a lovely little boy," she recalls.
"I was sad to have to say goodbye to him."

It must also have been a difficult situation
for the Tahany's, who had grown equally fond of
Augusta and Lino and who have, in fact, remained friends ever since, making regular visits
to *The Butcher's Arms*. In making arrangements for the parting of the ways,
Mr Tahany was more than fair and offered them a choice. They could either opt to go back
to Portugal, in which case he would pay all their expenses; or, if they decided to stay in
England, he would use his influence to find good jobs for both of them.

It didn't take them long to decide that they would stay. Both were still missing
their families terribly, especially Augusta, and yet they weren't quite ready to go back to
Portugal. It was partly pride. Lino had vowed before they set off for England that he would
not go back to Portugal until he could do so in style, having done well for himself. He
wanted to be able to return with his head held high. And so far he felt that he had not
done enough. Apart from that, both he and Augusta and grown to like England and were
in no doubt that it still offered more opportunities for them than Portugal.

So, they chose to stay. And when they told Mr Tahany of their decision he was as
good as his word, arranging jobs for them at his favourite hotel restaurant in the area,
the very posh *Three Horse Shoes* in Rugby.

Bacalhau
SALTED COD

Salted cod was just about the only fish I can remember eating in Paiágua, which was so far from the sea. It is so popular in Portugal that it is said to be the basis for 365 recipes, one for each day of the year.

SERVES 6

1 lb/450g salt cod (mostly sold in little wooden boxes)

5 to 6 large potatoes

2 large onions, sliced

1 green pepper, sliced into slivers

3 hard-boiled eggs, sliced

4 cloves of garlic, crushed

olives

black pepper to taste

2 tablespoons of parsley, chopped

juice of one lemon

olive oil

freshly ground black pepper

Soak the cod overnight. The following day gently poach it in unsalted water for 15 minutes. Flake the fish and set aside. Boil the potatoes, slice and set aside. Slice onion, pepper, crushed garlic and sauté in olive oil.

In a large casserole add a layer of potatoes, fish, sliced eggs, onion, sliced pepper, garlic and lemon juice. Sprinkle over the olives and parsley. Season with pepper.

Pour olive oil over the casserole. Cover and bake at 180C or 350F for half an hour to 45 minutes.

Chicken Piri Piri

This is one of the most famous dishes in all Portugal – and has become well known all over the world. Chillis originally came from Africa and it was Christopher Columbus who first brought some chilli seeds to back to Portugal from the New World. Traders then carried the seeds to the African colonies of Angola and Mozambique.

We never ate it in the village, chickens were kept for their eggs and only killed for soup when they were old. Chicken Piri Piri became popular when tourists started arriving on the Algarve. I started eating it in when we lived in Sintra. Now it is one of our most popular dishes at The Butchers Arms and I taught all our chefs how to cook it.

SERVES 4

4 chicken breasts or legs
(I prefer to keep the skin on as
it keeps the chicken moist)

FOR THE MARINADE
6 fresh red chillis, finely chopped
(or 2 teaspoons of minced chilli paste)

2 cloves of garlic, crushed
3fl oz/100ml olive oil
½ teaspoon oregano
½ teaspoon paprika
2 tablespoons lemon juice
salt and pepper

Crush the salt, garlic and chillis together in a pestle and mortar. Put into a bowl with the olive oil and other ingredients and mix well together.

Score the flesh of the chicken and rub in the marinade. Leave in the refrigerator for at least an hour or overnight.

The chicken can be cooked on a grill for 30 minutes, turning occasionally and basting regularly. Or cooked in a griddle pan for 2–3 minutes each side and then transferred to a roasting tray and roasted in the oven for 30 minutes until cooked through.

If you like to barbecue, place it on the grill for 10–15 minutes each side.

Bread and Butter Pudding

I always find it is best to use stale white bread, cut into thick slices for this dish.

SERVES 4

8 slices bread

1½ oz/40 g softened butter

1 pint/600 ml milk

4 oz/110g sugar

4 oz/110g raisins and sultanas

3 eggs, slightly beaten

Butter a shallow ovenproof baking dish. Trim the crusts off the bread and generously spread each slice with butter – on one side only. Line the bottom of the dish with slices of bread, butter-side-down, sprinkle over the fruit and half the sugar. Cover with another layer of bread butter-side-up. Beat the eggs and milk and pour over the bread. Sprinkle with the remaining sugar.

    Butter the shiny side of some foil and cover the dish. Cook in a bain marie in a hot oven for about 30 minutes or until the egg mixture is set. If you want you can remove the foil and cook for a further 10 minutes or so until the top is crisp and golden.

Part Five

Rugby

The Three Horse Shoes had a reputation as one of the best hotel restaurants anywhere outside London in the early sixties.

Eating out in style was still something of a luxury at that time and really top class restaurants were virtually non-existent outside the West End. However, growing post-war economic prosperity and, in particular, the booming car and engineering industries in the Coventry and Birmingham area meant that there was an increasing demand in the Midlands for fine dining facilities, with a quality of food and service on a par with what was on offer in the capital.

Recognising this trend, the owners of *The Three Horse Shoes*, which was ideally located in the heart of what was one of the Midlands' poshest residential areas, had imported the former restaurant manager of the Savoy Grill, Jack Spencer, along with a couple of the Savoy chefs and a team of Italian waiters, to bring a bit of West End style to the provinces. They managed this so successfully that the restaurant soon became a magnet for everybody who was anybody in the region.

For Augusta and Lino, Mr Tahany's ability to fix them up with jobs there, using his influence as a regular and a highly valued customer, was another key factor in their personal success story. In characteristically determined fashion, the couple seized the

The Three Horseshoes *often attracted visiting celebrities.*
Actor Kenneth More acknowledges an admiring crowd outside
the hotel in the 1960's. Jack Spencer can be seen over More's
right shoulder, wearing a dark suit.

opportunity with both hands, working with tireless enthusiasm to make the most of this lucky break. But life there was very hard.

"Although the boss was very professional, he was also a miserable, angry-tempered man," recalls Augusta. "He could freeze you with his look and I would often end up in tears, even though his wife, who was much kinder, would assure me that I had done nothing wrong, that it was just the way he was. He was also very mean. He would not allow us to have even a bottle of water, because he thought that if he let us drink his water, then maybe we would also start taking something else of his."

Despite this, Augusta and Lino did well. Lino was soon promoted from waiter to cocktail barman, charming the customers with his chatty manner, his fractured English and his ability to remember not only all their names but also their favourite tipples. Augusta, meanwhile, was kept busy servicing the hotel's nine bedrooms.

She also managed to earn a little bit of extra money by ironing shirts for Jack Spencer and his brother, Fred, who was also involved in the management by this time, having previously worked in the Caprice in London. Most of the staff wore drip-dry nylon shirts for convenience, but these tended to turn a yellowish colour after a time and never looked very fresh. Lino, on the other hand, always wore a crisp white cotton shirt, immaculately laundered and ironed by Augusta. Jack Spencer soon noticed the difference. "How do you get your shirts to look so good?" he asked.

"Augusta does them for me," explained Lino.

"Well, would she do them for me?" he inquired.

"Oh, yes! I'm sure she would be delighted," replied Lino confident, as ever, that the already hard-pressed Augusta would be happy to oblige.

Soon everybody wanted her to do their shirts and Augusta would find herself taking home a dozen or more every Friday night. "I would wash them all by hand, "she remembers. "All I had was a spin dryer, not a hot air dryer. I would iron them all on a Saturday. My neighbour said that my house was like a Chinese laundry!" she remembers. And on top of that, she still found time to bake Jack Spencer a cake every weekend, purely out of the kindness of her heart.

For the first few months, she and Lino had been living in a dingy rented room just down the road from the hotel, but with their combined wages and tips amounting to nearly £20-a-week following Lino's promotion to barman, and with the additional help of an interest-free loan from the financial director of the company that owned *The Three Horse Shoes*, they were able to buy their first house – a semi in Lowford Road, Rugby for which they paid £2,000. At the same time, they decided they could afford to start a longed-for family.

Augusta was overjoyed when she fell pregnant almost immediately, only to suffer the trauma and heartbreak of a miscarriage after just a few weeks. Her doctor suspected that this may have been caused by all the running up and down stairs and the exertions involved in making beds, turning mattresses and cleaning out nine rooms every day and he advised her to give up work next time. This she did, even though the reduction in income put the family finances under considerable pressure.

Her son, Peter, was born at St Mary's Hospital, Rugby on February 4th, 1964 after several hours' hard labour. "It was not an easy birth. I can't imagine why there are so many people in the world when women have to go through such agony," jokes Augusta, recalling the experience with a grimace. "Once was quite enough for me!"

Despite all the discomfort, it was the proudest and most fulfilling moment of her life when she held her baby in her arms for the first time. Did she shed a few tears? Of course she did! But for perhaps the first time since she had left home, they were tears of pure happiness As for Lino, he was like a dog with two tails, immediately making plans for a triumphant return to Paiágua to show off his son and heir and to flaunt his success now that things were starting to go so well.

It took nearly a week for news of Peter's birth to reach the village by post, still the only available means of communication. Four months later, as soon as he was old enough to fly, he was taken over to make his first personal appearance. Lino had already shipped out his other pride and joy – a very second-hand turquoise Ford Capri – so that the family could make a grand entrance. A son and a car! Here was a man who had definitely made his mark!

The highlight of their month-long visit was Peter's christening in the little chapel at Paiágua where his parents had been married seven years earlier. The ceremony was

A son and a car! Here was a man who had definitely made his mark! (Top) The turquoise Ford Capri in
which the family made a triumphant return to Paiágua, Augusta with Peter and Peter himself in classic pose.

Family snapshots from a
later return visit to Paiágua.
Peter with Lino's mother (left),
perched on the donkey on
which Augusta's father used
to ride to work (top left) and
(middle) with other members
of the family.

attended by all the members of the two families, friends and most of the village. And for the rest of their stay, which they divided between the two sets of in-laws, they were the centre of attention, with lots of parties and re-unions and everybody wanting to know about every detail of their lives in England.

For Augusta, there were many highly emotional moments during the visit, but also some mixed feelings. It was wonderful for her to be back among her family, having not seen or spoken to them for four long years. And yet, as she learned to live again in houses without any of the modern conveniences that she had now got used to in England, she realised that there was no point in trying to pretend that she would ever be going back permanently. She and Lino had spent years trying to get away and now that they had succeeded there could be no turning back. They might not always remain quite so far away, but even if they did return to live and work in Portugal one day, it would be to Lisbon, not to Paiágua. It was noticeable that more and more of the younger generation were starting to move away to the towns and cities. The exodus was destined to develop from a trickle to a flood in the years to come, many family homes becoming deserted once the old folk died off and, with no newcomers to buy them, gradually falling into disrepair and then dereliction. Others would be maintained only as occasional holiday homes. All this was still some way off in 1964, but for Augusta the sad truth was that her beloved Paiágua was already beginning to seem like part of a past life.

Even so, it was a terrible wrench for her when, at the end of the month's stay that ended all too quickly, she had to say goodbye again and head back to England. Lino drove them back in the Ford, a journey of 1,500 miles. It took just two days – an indication of how little traffic there was in those days – but for Augusta, who has never had the greatest confidence in Lino's driving skills, it seemed like a fortnight! "I didn't see much of the scenery – I had my eyes shut most of the time," she recalls with a shudder.

Back at *The Three Horse Shoes*, she had to reduce her hours so that she could look after Peter. She would get up at five o'clock in the morning and work only until 9.00 am before going back to the house to take over from Lino, who would have been baby-sitting in her absence, so that he could then go into work. At 5.00pm she would then return to the hotel to turn the beds down, getting home back just in time for Lino to go off and open up the bar for the evening. One way another, they saw very little of each other.

Meanwhile, big changes were afoot in the hotel itself. Only a few months after Lino and Augusta returned from Portugal, Jack Spencer announced that he was leaving to start a place of his own. With financial backing from the group that owned *The Three Horse Shoes*, he had bought a run down pub called *The Bowling Green*, just off the market square in Warwick, which he did up and then re-opened as *The Westgate Arms*. Under his expert management, this soon took over from *The Three Horse Shoes* as the No 1 restaurant in the area, with most of his customers gradually following him from Rugby to Warwick.

Lino was desperate to go with him – and Jack was equally keen to have him. The problem was that under the terms of the financial arrangement Jack had with the owners of *The Three Horse Shoes* he was contractually bound not to poach any of the staff, especially Lino himself, for a period of three years. In the end, increasingly frustrated by the decline in standards in the restaurant following Jack's departure and the rapid defection of all his favourite cocktail bar customers, Lino effectively delivered an

Olga Maruso (old friend from Portugal)

'For more than 40 years I have lived and worked in England and it is all thanks
to Augusta and Lino. My late husband worked with Lino in Portugal and
it was he and Augusta who suggested we came to Rugby to work with them at
The Three Horseshoes.

Augusta was a wonderful chambermaid, such a hard worker and I really enjoyed
working with her. She was also fun, she would make me laugh. I was not surprised
the bosses really respected her and Lino, they are such good, kind people.

They not only looked after me when I came to England, they helped teach me the
language. I went on to become the housekeeper at the hotel, so I owe them a lot. '

The Westgate Arms in Warwick in the 1960s

ultimatum to the chairman of the board. He was going to leave anyway, he said, so it made sense for them to let him go to a place in which they had a financial interest rather than to some other rival establishment. It worked, and a month later he and Augusta moved to Warwick.

Having sold their house in Rugby, they rented a flat just down the road from *The Westgate Arms*.

However, the new job didn't work out quite as expected, because instead of being in the cocktail bar, Lino found himself put in charge of the Town Bar, a public bar that was totally separate from the restaurant. This was not at all what he had had in mind. Isolated from the sort of up-market clientele with whom he had established such a rapport at *The Three Horse Shoes*, he was very unhappy in his work, which involved washing up all the glasses from the restaurant and the cocktail bar as well as from the Town Bar itself, a chore that would often keep him there until two o'clock in the morning. Apart from that, there was absolutely no opportunity to earn the generous tips that were on offer in the cocktail bar.

While Augusta was enjoying the opportunity to be a full-time mum, Lino was becoming more and more frustrated with the routine at the Westgate. His thoughts turned again to finding a place of his own and as a first step he wrote off to all the major breweries in search of a pub tenancy. What he really wanted was a nice little country pub, but what he was eventually offered was *The Railway Inn*, a back street boozer in a scruffy commercial area of Leicester.

As soon as she set eyes on the place, Augusta's face fell and her heart sank. It was awful. Not only was it located in a most unattractive part of the city, close to the railway station and right opposite the GPO headquarters; it was also dirty and grimy and in dire need of redecoration, inside and out, after years of neglect. By the time they had finished looking round the gloomy Victorian premises, where everything was covered in dark brown paint, Augusta was in total despair. She couldn't understand why Lino would even consider swapping the security of his reasonably well-paid job at the Westgate and the comfort of their nice little flat in St John's Court for such a dreadful place, especially as it seemed to have so little potential. The two of them rowed about it so fiercely in the car that at one point Lino lost concentration and backed into a wall as he was turning round.

Augusta knew that he wouldn't be put off. He was very ambitious and his long-term aim had always been to have his own business. He wasn't interested in being a waiter or a barman for the rest of his life. They had to start somewhere, he argued, and although *The Railway Inn* represented a very lowly beginning, it at least gave them a foothold. Trust me, he said. And, of course, she did. As with all the big decisions that have been made throughout their time together, she left it to Lino and then, however much she feared that he might have made a terrible mistake, backed him to the hilt, labouring overtime to make the most of the situation.

The Railway Inn provided a classic example of how Lino and Augusta work perfectly together as a team. It truly was a pretty dreadful place when they took over. A real spit-and-sawdust working man's pub, it catered almost exclusively for the GPO workers from across the road who would descend en masse during their breaks and at the end of each shift, fighting to get to the bar first and swilling pints of mild and bitter as fast as possible. The rest of the time, it was empty. There was no food available and you would rarely, if ever, see a woman there.

Gradually, however, the combination of Lino's charm and Augusta's cooking helped to bring about a transformation. The introduction of home-made bar snacks such as gammon and egg and chicken casserole attracted a slightly different crowd and the fact that people were sitting down to eat at the new tables that the brewery had been persuaded to provide, once Lino and Augusta had first cleaned the place up a bit, produced a subtle change in atmosphere. It was no longer quite such a roughhouse and Lino was able to persuade one or two of the GPO people to bring their wives and girlfriends in for a meal in the evenings and at weekends. And whereas the place had previously been deserted on Saturday and Sunday nights, it suddenly started to become quite busy. Within a few months The Railway Inn had built a reputation as one of the better pubs in town and the weekly takings had soared from £120 to £800.

Despite this remarkable turnaround, Lino and Augusta could see that there was no long-term future there. They had never had any intention of being there longer than they had to be and a pub like that was certainly no place in which to bring up a young child. When the GPO then started work on a new twenty-storey office block right next door, the resulting noise, mess and general inconvenience threatened to undermine the flourishing business they had built up, convincing them that they ought to move sooner rather than later.

Hugely impressed by the success they had made of *The Railway Inn*, the brewery were quick to offer them the pick of their tenancies, but Lino had now made up his mind that he was only interested in a freehold property, where he and Augusta would be working purely for themselves. However, that would have to wait until they had built up a bit more capital. In the meantime, he decided to return temporarily to *The Westgate*. He had been badly missed there, so he was not only welcomed back with open arms but was also able to put pressure on Jack Spencer to let him take over in the cocktail bar, where he would once again be in his element. At the same time, Augusta was also given a job, looking after the ladies' cloakroom and also helping out in the restaurant.

The extra profits made from Augusta's cooking at *The Railway Inn* provided the down payment on a very nice £3,000 house in Warwick, just a few minutes' walk from *The Westgate*. And with Lino earning good money in the cocktail bar and Augusta also working, they could afford to send Peter to private nursery school at Emscote Lawn. Having had so little education themselves, Lino and Augusta were determined to make sure that their son should have the best. Peter was only four years old, but Lino already had his eye on Rugby. While working at *The Three Horse Shoes* he had been shown round the school by a master to whom he'd got chatting one night when serving him in the bar there and from that moment on he had dreamed of being able to send Peter there.

The four years that Augusta and Lino spent at *The Westgate* between 1968 and 1972

Rugby School – only the best would do.

were frantically busy, with little time for family life together. With Augusta working during the day and Lino on duty at lunchtime and again in the evening, often until the early hours, they only seemed to see each other in passing. They developed a relay system of school runs and general child-minding, one taking over from the other to fit in with their complicated daily timetable. It wasn't ideal, but they told themselves that it wouldn't go on like that for ever. Eventually, they would have a place of their own and then things would be different.

Lino constantly had his eye out for a suitable pub, guest house, small hotel or bed & breakfast place. Along with his cousin Eric, who had been brought over from Portugal at Lino's suggestion to work as a waiter at *The Westgate*, he travelled as far afield as Wales and Dorset on his days off to look at various possibilities, none of which were quite right. At one stage he got as far as arranging a mortgage for a small hotel that came up for sale in Leamington Spa, but the deal fell through at the last moment when a building society search revealed Council plans to build a roundabout on the site!

It was shortly after this disappointment that Lino came home from *The Westgate* in the early hours of a Sunday morning in a state of high excitement and woke Augusta to announce that he had just bought a country pub.

Pat Owen (customer and friend):

. . . .

‘ I first met Augusta and Lino when my parents, who were regular customers, took me to The Westgate Hotel. I remember Augusta being very touched when my mother, Betty Shortland, gave her a present of her favourite perfume that Augusta had once noticed her wearing and had greatly admired.

My husband David and I have 100 per cent admiration for what Lino and Augusta have achieved, especially considering that they came to this country not even speaking English. Through sheer hard work and determination they have built up their business into one of the most successful restaurants in the Midlands.

And they have done it by working together as a team, both totally dedicated to their job. While Lino is the perfect front man, Augusta is the one whizzing away in the background, all the time being totally supportive of Lino.

She is such a helpful, considerate and caring person. When our now grown-up daughter, Camilla, was a baby, we would take her with us when we went for lunch on Sundays and Augusta would kindly take her upstairs into her bedroom so that we could enjoy lunch.

It's no wonder that all our family celebrations for the past thirty years have been at The Butcher's Arms. We truly feel that we are all part of Lino and Augusta's family. ’

. . . .

Marmelo
QUINCE JAM

The Portuguese name for quince is Marmelo, which is where the word marmalade came from and until two hundred years ago marmalade was always made from quinces and not oranges. We used to make it every year. I love the smell of quinces, but don't try eating them unless they are cooked, the flesh is very bitter when raw.

> 2 lbs / 900g quinces, prepared weight
> 1½ pints / 900ml water
> 2 tablespoons lemon juice
> 3 lbs /1.3 kg granulated or preserving sugar

Peel, core, slice and then weigh the quinces. Place in a pan with the water and lemon juice. Simmer very gently with the lid on until really soft and mushy. (Reduce a little if needed by boiling with the lid off). Add the sugar and stir well until dissolved. Then boil rapidly until setting point is reached. Pot and cover in the usual way.

Quince Cheese

We also made this quince cheese – which is not a cheese at all but a solid fruit preserve that goes particularly well with manchego cheese. It makes a great combination of tastes.

> 2.2 lb/ 1kg. preserving sugar
> 1¼ pint/750 ml water
> 2.2 lb/1 kg quince, peeled, cored and grated or cut into small pieces

Dissolve the sugar in the water and bring to the boil. Continue to boil for about 5 minutes to make a light syrup. Stir the quince into the syrup, bring back to the boil and simmer very gently, stirring every so often, for anything from 45 minutes to 1½ hours until the mixture turns into a thick grainy paste. This is a slow process and there's nothing for it but patience but I find giving it an occasional whisk helps the process along. It is ready when the spoon, dragged across the bottom of the pan, separates the paste, showing the clean bottom of the pan.

Spread the paste into lightly greased shallow dishes or trays and place in the oven at its lowest possible temperature for 3-4 hours to harden further. Remove from the oven and leave to cool. Once cool, wrap in greaseproof paper in useable slabs that you can give away as gifts or keep for your own use. Store these in the fridge in sealed containers. It will keep for up to a year.

Chicken Casserole

I used to make this when we had The Railway Inn in Leicester. It was hugely popular.

SERVES 4

8 chicken portions (thighs or legs)

selection of vegetables (such as carrots, potatoes, parsnips,
    swedes, courgettes, shallots)

9 fl oz/250ml white wine (optional)

9 fl oz/250ml water

9 fl oz/250ml chicken stock (or 18 fl oz/500 ml if not using wine)

fresh herbs (such as parsley or thyme)

freshly ground black pepper and salt

Remove the skin from the chicken if you prefer and place it in a large lidded casserole dish. Peel and dice/slice the vegetables. As a general rule, the harder the vegetable, the smaller you should dice it as it will take longer to cook. Potatoes and swedes should be diced small. Softer vegetables such as courgettes should be sliced thickly.

Scatter the vegetables over the chicken, and add the stock, wine and water. Chop the fresh herbs and add them. Finally, season with salt and pepper.

Place the lid on the casserole and cook in a moderately hot oven for 1½ to 2 hours or until the chicken and vegetables are cooked through.

Tomato Rice

I love this recipe. We would cook this in Paiágua — and I always did it by feel, I never measured anything out. But for this recipe I've measured everything carefully, just to make sure it will work for you as it always does for me!

SERVES 4

4 medium tomatoes (skinned)
1 medium sized onion, finely chopped
1 sprig parsley
1 sprig thyme
2 tablespoons olive oil
1¾ pint/1 litre water
2 chicken stock cubes
12 oz/350 g long grain rice
salt and freshly ground black pepper

Heat the oil and soften the onions in a large pot. Add the skinned and chopped tomatoes, thyme and parsley. Add the water and stock cubes. Check for seasoning. Add a pinch of salt and the pepper. When the liquid boils add the rice, reduce to a simmer, cover the pot and allow the rice to cook until it has absorbed all of the liquid

Christmas Pudding

We were living in Warwick in 1966 when we bought our first electric cooker. With it came a cookery book and I worked my way through it, making many of the recipes — some of them subsequently appeared on the menu at The Butchers Arms. My recipe for Christmas pudding came from that old book and I have never found a better one.

3 oz/85g flour

3 oz/85g fresh breadcrumbs

4 oz/115g chopped suet

4 oz/115g sugar

½ level teaspoon salt

1 level teaspoon mixed spice

pinch of grated nutmeg

12 oz/350g mixed dried fruit
  (currants, raisins, sultanas)

2 oz/55g chopped peel

1 oz/30g glace cherries (chopped)

2 oz/55g chopped almonds

juice and grated rind of one lemon

2 eggs

2 tablespoons brandy

Mix flour, breadcrumbs, suet, sugar, salt, mixed spice and nutmeg together in a large bowl. Add prepared dried fruit, chopped peel, cherries, almonds and grated lemon rind. Beat the eggs and stir them into the dry ingredients. Add brandy and lemon juice. Mix well. The mixture should be quite soft. Add a little milk if necessary. Turn into a greased basin. Cover with greased paper and pudding cloth. Tie down tightly. Steam or boil for 4 hours. Remove pudding cloth and cover with greased paper and clean cloth for storing. When re-heating steam or boil for at least one hour before serving.

Augusta's original Christmas Pudding recipe.

Part Six

Priors Hardwick

Augusta can laugh about it now, but when she first set eyes on The Butcher's Arms she once again burst into tears.

A run-down village pub, it appeared to her to be just as awful as *The Railway Inn* in many ways and she experienced the same sinking feeling when she was shown around the place the morning after Lino had agreed to buy it, unseen, from a customer he happened to get chatting to in the cocktail bar of *The Westgate Arms*.

Priors Hardwick was certainly a much prettier spot than downtown Leicester, but the pub itself was just as drab and dilapidated. Dating back to 1375, the building may have had an interesting history, but the rooms were dark and gloomy, the bars were cramped and when Augusta saw the pokey little kitchen, its one small, domestic cooker covered in grease and grime, she nearly had a fit. It looked as if it hadn't been properly cleaned since the Civil War, when the inn had become a Royalist stronghold on the eve of the Battle of Edge Hill in 1642. Was this where she was going to be expected to produce the sort of meals that would lure discerning customers away from *The Westgate*? She gazed round in speechless horror.

Lino, as ever, was totally up-beat about his impulsive purchase – although he admits now that he, too, had misgivings. He didn't let this show at the time. They'd soon get the place in order, he insisted confidently. A country pub was what they had always wanted and, although far from perfect in some respects, this one had bags of potential.

The Butcher's Arms *as it was when Augusta first saw it.*

What's more, the price was exactly right, just within the bounds of what they could afford. Once he had established that, the only other thing Lino had wanted to know in advance from the vendor was whether it was in Warwickshire?

That was important to him because he knew that most of his potential *Westgate Arms* customer base lived in Warwickshire and he didn't want to stray too far out of their area. Once assured that the pub was indeed within the county boundary, he shook hands on a deal there and then. Only at that point did he bother to ask *exactly* where it was located.

Already apprehensive from the moment Lino came home and told her what he had done, Augusta became even more anxious when they drove out from Warwick to have a look at the property. For a start, they were unable to find it, despite being armed with a sketch map given to Lino by the man he had bought it from. They got to Priors Hardwick all right, but then took the wrong turn into the village and somehow missed the pub altogether. "If we can't find it even with the directions we've been given, how will our customers ever find their way there?" sobbed Augusta, as they drove round in circles, ending up in Priors Marston, the neighbouring village.

"It will be fine," promised Lino confidently. "Trust me."

And, as always, she did.

They moved in on New Year's Day, 1973. While Lino went on ahead in the car,

The Butcher's Arms *as it looks today.*

Augusta travelled with Peter in the removals van, which first got lost and then ran aground on a hump back bridge on the road leading into Priors Hardwick, convincing Augusta once again that nobody in their right mind would ever venture so far out into the sticks to eat. But once they had settled in, she put all doubts aside in characteristic fashion and threw herself into the job of making a success of the venture.

The story of those early years at *The Butcher's Arms* is one of Lino's vision, enterprise and drive and Augusta's skill, dedication and endless hard work. Although it was not exactly 'open all hours', *The Butcher's Arms* stretched the licensing laws to the very limit. And then, as now, Lino could never bear to turn away anybody who wanted a meal, whatever the time of day. As a result, the pub soon became a favourite with the local Young Farmers Club fraternity, who would often start to feel peckish at the end of a heavy night's drinking.

Half-a-dozen steak and chips and three ham and eggs ordered five minutes before closing time? No problem, Lino would reply without hesitation. And Augusta, who had probably closed the kitchen down an hour earlier, would don her apron and start cooking all over again, often carrying on until midnight. If she ever grumbled, Lino would teasingly accuse her of being like the Mona Lisa – "because you moan a lot!" The truth was that, underneath it all, Augusta never really minded the hard work; she was as keen as he was to make a success of the place.

Meanwhile, the young farmers soon found themselves rubbing shoulders with captains of industry and other VIPs as the many good friends that the couple had made among the Westgate's up-market clientele did indeed make the effort to venture off the beaten track to Priors Hardwick. They came at first out of loyalty and because they were curious to see how things were going, but soon found the combination of Lino's welcoming charm and Augusta's simple but delicious home cooking to be irresistible. As a result, the reputation of *The Butcher's Arms* as the best pub restaurant for miles around spread throughout the county and beyond, prompting more and more people to come and see what all the fuss was about. As business boomed, with takings rising from £2,700 to more than £20,000 in the first year, Lino set about extending the restaurant.

Over the years, it has gradually spread outwards in all directions – a sort of creeping development that started with the enlargement of the original bar and dining area, the modernisation of the kitchen and the building of indoor toilets. This was followed by the addition of what now forms the main restaurant. Further extensions at fairly regular intervals between 1973 and 2001 included the ever-expanding coffee lounge and the conservatory. Business would always carry on as usual while these alterations were being carried out, the builders often moving in after Sunday lunch and then working throughout the night so that the restaurant could open as usual for lunch the next day.

Augusta found the regular disruptions extremely stressful, especially as she was not always entirely convinced that Lino's latest 'improvement' was absolutely necessary. To avoid any arguments, he would often send her off on holiday to see her family and friends in Portugal without telling her what he had planned and she would come back to be faced by a

Augusta shortly after she and Lino moved to The Butcher's Arms. Business boomed straightaway, with takings rising from £2,700 to £20,000 in their first year.

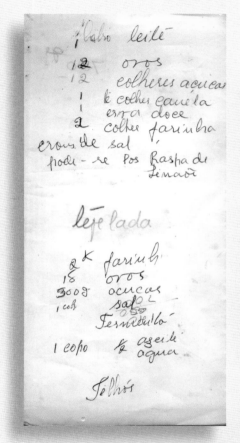

The menu soon included many dishes made to Augusta's own distinctive recipes.

fait accompli. One member of staff recalls: "When Augusta went off on holiday on her own you always knew that the place was about to be ripped apart again to find some way of fitting in a few more tables."

As Lino enlarged the restaurant to accommodate even more customers, so Augusta extended the menu. As well as standard pub fare such as steak and chips, gammon, scampi and ham and eggs, she started offering traditional Portuguese dishes, including marinated chicken and chicken with chilli, plus soups, stews, casseroles and then Sunday roasts. Desserts included Portuguese rice pudding, bread-and-butter pudding and profiteroles, all made to her own distinctive recipes. Gradually, she became more and more adventurous, adding all the main classic dishes to her repertoire. Completely self taught, she simply worked from cookbooks, while also making use of tips she had picked up from watching the chefs at *The Three Horse Shoes* and *The Westgate*. And the results soon came to be regarded by discerning diners as the equal of anything they had eaten at either of those two establishments, if not better.

For the first two years after *The Butcher's Arms* opened, Augusta did all the cooking herself – and most of the washing up as well! Mollie Ward, Margaret Hobbs and Helen Sadiq, three of the wives among the earliest regular customers, nearly all of whom ended up becoming close personal friends of Lino and Augusta, would often get up at the end of a meal and go into the kitchen to give Augusta a hand with the dishes. They were genuinely worried that she was in danger of working herself to death. "You mustn't worry about Augusta," Lino re-assured them. "She is much stronger than you think. And don't imagine for one moment that I don't appreciate everything that she does. Nobody could love and value her more than I do. She knows that, and although she complains about the way I am always trying to push ahead, she wouldn't want me to do things any differently. We are both in this together."

By 1975, however, the restaurant was so busy, catering for an average of one hundred covers every day, that Augusta clearly couldn't go on any longer doing everything herself and so Lino sent back to Portugal and brought over Francisco Simao, the son of a childhood friend, to help out in the kitchen. Known to one and all as Simon, Francisco remained at *The Butcher's Arms* for twenty-seven years and ended up as head chef, having been trained up from scratch by Augusta. She taught him everything he knew and although he became very good indeed, there were one or two dishes that he could never do quite as well as she did. One regular customer – the Pires family GP, Dr Peter Middleton – recalls that he and his wife would deliberately book to eat at the restaurant on nights when they knew the chef was off duty, just so that they would have the chance to savour Augusta's cooking.

The professionals have been equally impressed by her culinary skills. Celebrity chef Tony Tobin, who grew up in the next village, worked as a kitchen boy at *The Butcher's Arms* during his school holidays and it was this experience that inspired him to become a chef himself. When he was accepted at the local catering college, Augusta and Lino went out and bought him his first set of professional kitchen knives. Now with his own restaurant in Reigate, Surrey, Tony still goes back to eat at *The Butcher's Arms* whenever he is in the area and waxes lyrical at the memory of some of Augusta's specialities, such as pate, steak and kidney pie and profiteroles. "Whenever I smell steak and kidney pie I'm instantly wafted back to my days at *The Butcher's Arms*," he recalls fondly.

Dion van Overdijk, who took over as head chef from Francisco Simao, remembers how Augusta would carefully road test any new recipes that were suggested before then adapting them to suit the tastes of her clientele, which she knew precisely. "In the end, I learned never to argue with her about how any dish should be prepared because she was nearly always right," he says.

As the restaurant started to take off, extra waiters were brought in, nearly all of them Portuguese and most of them members of Augusta's or Lino's family. First to arrive was Augusta's nephew Eric, followed later by Eric's brother, José. Then there was Lino's cousin Adriano and his wife, Laurinda. Like Simon, the chef, Adriano stayed for more than twenty years. Right from the start, the familiar presence of long-serving staff members has helped to create and maintain the family atmosphere that has always been such an important ingredient in the success of *The Butcher's Arms*.

The other key factor has always been the very special relationship that exists between Lino and Augusta and their customers. At *The Butcher's Arms*, the couple are now serving the fourth generation of some families that they first encountered in their days at

Front of house: Augusta and Lino with the restaurant staff at The Butcher's Arms.

Fan mail – customers, including some very famous ones, are often moved to write to Augusta and Lino to let them know just how much they enjoyed the experience of dining at The Butcher's Arms.

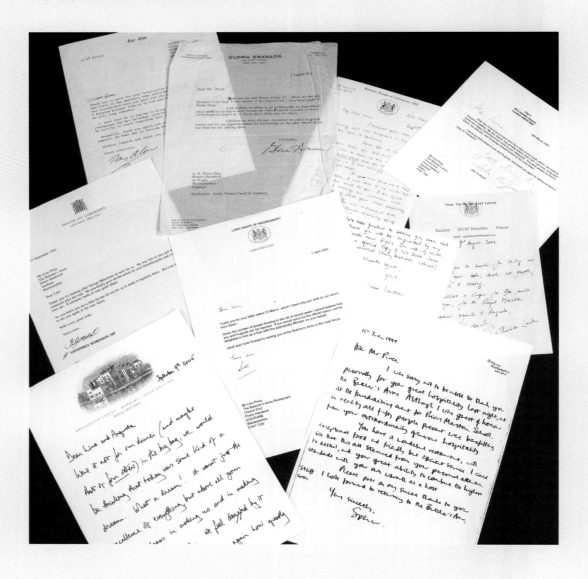

The Three Horse Shoes and The Westgate. And that kind of loyalty cannot be explained by good food alone. They exude a genuine warmth and friendliness that reaches out beyond the confines of the restaurant itself, and stories of their generosity and their many gestures of support and kindness are legendary.

Peter and Helen in the bar,
where there's always a hearty welcome.

What's more, there is a something about their rock solid family values – especially now that their son Peter and his wife Helen are also such an integral part of the business – that is as comforting and reliable as the wonderfully traditional food they serve. Lino and Augusta work side-by-side in a way that is only possible when a couple have been operating together as a team for so long that they become like two halves of a whole. They complement each other perfectly. Lino is the consummate front-of-house man, happy to admit that he can hardly boil an egg and yet a past master at the art of meeting and greeting and making every first-time customer feel instantly at home – particularly the ladies! – while Augusta is very happy to remain in the background, quietly running the whole show behind the scenes.

When asked for a comment to be included in Lino's autobiography, Lord Lawson, the former Conservative Chancellor and a regular customer for many years, went out of his way to stress: "Don't forget Augusta, she's a very important part of this success story." As well as keeping a supervisory eye on the kitchen and still doing some of the cooking herself, she is also the one who does all the flower arrangements, who checks the tables in advance to make sure that every napkin is perfectly folded and every glass sparklingly clean and who then directs operations from her little office between the kitchen and the dining room.

And although every bit as shy as Lino is extrovert, she does like to pop out into the restaurant every now and again for a quick chat with those customers she knows best and with whom she feels most comfortable, often delighting them with some extremely risqué joke, the punch line accompanied by that distinctive, earthy laugh. Or she may suddenly become very emotional, the tears welling up at the mere mention of some fond family memory or sad recollection. With Augusta, sunshine and showers are never far apart. That is an endearing part of her personality.

Thirty-four years after she and Lino started serving up ham and eggs in a tiny back bar where there was barely room for half-a-dozen small tables, the restaurant now routinely caters for up to two hundred customers during a busy evening or Sunday lunchtime. The walls are lined with photographs of the rich and famous who have eaten there over the years, many of them on a regular basis. They include film and television personalities, sportsmen, top politicians and business tycoons. They come for the food, of course. But what also draws them is the very special, homely atmosphere. And at the heart and soul of that atmosphere are Lino and – more than is perhaps immediately obvious – Augusta.

The wall of fame in the coffee lounge – from Ian Botham to one of the men on the moon, they've all visited The Butcher's Arms *at some time or another.*

Dion Van Overdijk (Former head chef, Butchers Arms):
....

❛ They say that behind every great man there is a great woman and
this is definitely true of Lino and Augusta. Where Lino has the charm and the
flair, Augusta has the eye for detail. She demands consistency from
all the staff and leads by example.

During almost twelve years at the Butchers Arms I learned much
about economising, about the importance of using only produce of the highest
quality and of showing loyalty to long-term suppliers. The worst thing
about my occasional battles of will with Augusta was the fact that
she was nearly always right.

Any new recipes that we introduced were carefully scrutinized and often adapted
to suit the acquired tastes of the clientele, which Augusta knew so well. It took
me some time to accept her guidance, but later came to realise that she had
obviously seen and done it all before.

Because Augusta is a diabetic she should not consume sugar. However, sweets
have always been her nemesis and her one vice is raiding the sweet fridges. Often
the staff played ignorant as to where some of the desserts may have gone. At one
stage we had to replace the sweet fridges and, as it happened, they had locks on
the doors. When Augusta noticed this, she asked us to make sure that the doors
were locked in the afternoon and the key hidden, so that she wouldn't be able to
get in even if she was tempted. But then, only two days later,

she asked if she could please have a spare key, just in case some
customers showed up in the afternoon.

It is true that a lot of chefs behave like prima donnas and throw the odd
wobbly, but I have to admit that whenever Augusta went on a well deserved
break to her house in Portugal, I couldn't wait for her to return.
Somehow her absence created a 'freedom' that many members of staff
could never cope with very well.

Augusta was always so keen for the staff to get on with each other that she
would go out of her way to encourage this. I remember one Sunday evening
when Lino, Rogerio (a Portuguese waiter), Mick, (a Polish chef) and myself
(a Dutchman) were playing a Portuguese game in the car park. Augusta
provided wine for all of us – and I got the largest glass! Later I arrived home
somewhat the worse for wear, walking my bike, with the front wheel the wrong
way round, my elbows grazed and my legs covered in nettle stings having
ridden into the ditch. I'm 6'4" and weigh over 18 stone, but Augusta told me
off like a naughty little boy and made sure I only drunk water the next day. **❯**

Helen Sadiq (Longtime customer and close friend):

....

❛ For several years, Augusta and I went regularly to Champney's Health Farm
together. It was very much her treat, after working so hard all year round,
and it was wonderful to see her relaxing for once. She adored the treatments
and the swimming pool.

Of course, being a health farm, alcohol was forbidden, but that
didn't stop Augusta.

The first time we went there together, she told me: 'I'll bring the wine'.

On the way there, we then realised we'd forgotten a corkscrew and made a
detour to Tesco's in Tring to buy one. We then sat sipping our illicit glasses of
wine in our bedroom, feeling like naughty schoolgirls.

Whenever she gets the chance, she loves to have fun. I especially remember one
New Year's Eve at The Butcher's Arms. After all the other customers had left,

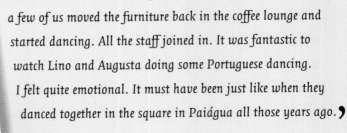

a few of us moved the furniture back in the coffee lounge and
started dancing. All the staff joined in. It was fantastic to
watch Lino and Augusta doing some Portuguese dancing.
I felt quite emotional. It must have been just like when they
danced together in the square in Paiágua all those years ago. ❜

....

John Sadiq (Longtime customer and close friend):

....

‘ *Augusta has the most wonderful, earthy sense of humour and a lovely infectious laugh. She loves to tell us the latest joke she has heard — and some of them are quite outrageous, although always very funny. When she delivers the punch line she laughs uproariously and then often looks rather embarrassed, blushing scarlet and clamping a hand over her mouth to stifle her giggles before turning away and sweeping out of the room with a swish of her skirts, leaving us chuckling away.* ’

....

Rosemary Green (Longtime customer and friend):

....

‘ *When my sons were very young, all the desserts on the sweet trolley were made by Augusta herself. Going to The Butchers Arms was always a highlight in our lives — most anniversaries, all my sons’ birthdays and also the night before they returned to school at the start of each new term. When Augusta knew the boys were coming in she always made a point of putting some chocolate profiteroles to one side, because she knew how much the boys loved them. Recently, I took my youngest son, Ryan, for dinner there to celebrate his 30th birthday — and, much to his surprise, and delight, Augusta came out bearing a chocolate profiterole cake — baked just for him.* ’

....

A holiday job as a washer up in the kitchen at The Butcher's Arms
when he was a schoolboy proved to be an inspiration for celebrity chef Tony Tobin.

Tony Tobin (Celebrity chef and
Chef Patron of The Dining Room in Reigate, Surrey):

. . . .

❛ I started working at The Butcher's Arms as a washer-upper when I was 13.
At the end of each night Augusta would push the sweet trolley back into the
kitchen and we would help ourselves — I'd usually have a little trifle, a few
profiteroles and maybe some chocolate éclairs. She was very fond of me and
looked after me so well. I suppose I was a bit of a teacher's pet!
One Christmas Day, after we'd been working flat out on Christmas lunch, we all
sat down around five o'clock to enjoy our Christmas meal. Everyone that
worked for Lino and Augusta was treated like family, and not just at
Christmas. But on this occasion Augusta gave me a little taste of her favourite
wine — the sparkling Alianca rosé. I was only 14 at the time, it was my first
taste of wine and when she saw that I clearly enjoyed it, she giggled: "Oh, look
at Tony, he just loves it! He already knows what is nice!"
I learnt an enormous amount from Augusta. When I arrived at The Butchers
Arms she was still making all the cold starters herself. I can still vividly
remember the smell of the liver paté that she used to make. It was lovely — and
hugely popular. She would serve it in such generous portions that people would
often take home what they couldn't eat, wrapped up in a napkin.
I still pop in whenever I'm in the area and get welcomed back like
a long-lost son. ❜

. . . .

Susan Moore (Longtime customer and friend):

....

❛ Augusta is so full of fun that she can still make you smile, even when
she is not feeling so well herself.

The whole family, several generations of us, have been going to The Butcher's
Arms since the early days. Augusta always likes to make a big fuss of us and
loves sharing a joke with my husband, John. On one occasion we were sitting at
the table, celebrating John's uncle's birthday, when Augusta approached and
gave John a gift bag. He explained that it wasn't his birthday, but she insisted
that she had bought the present especially for him. He peered rather nervously
inside the bag, because he knows her of old. She stood back to watch, waiting to
see his reaction, but John lost his nerve and said he would open it later.

"No," insisted Augusta. "Now! Now!"

John was so worried about the surprise that might be in store that he made
me open it. I reached in a pulled out a black silk man's thong.

John's face went bright red, while the whole table erupted in cheers.

Meantime, Augusta sauntered off, crying with laughter.

Everybody also knows how thoughtful and kind-hearted she is. When I worked
in the Ladies Wear department of Rackhams in Leamington Spa twenty years
ago, Augusta was one of my favourite customers. She bought a lot of her clothes
from me in those days and I am sure that she only bought some of those things
because she thought I was on commission – although I never was.

Our sons, who have grown up enjoying many Butcher's Arms' meals over the years, once popped in to the restaurant while John and I were having a meal with my parents. They had come just for a drink before saying their goodbyes. Some time later I popped out to the loo and saw my boys sitting in the bar while Augusta plied them with platefuls of food. She obviously couldn't bear to think they would leave without eating. They were having an absolute ball. She shooed me away, laughing and saying: "Nothing to do with you! Go away!" **)**

'Augusta always likes to make a big fuss of us,' says Susan (far right).

Jenny Hayward (Customer since The Westgate Hotel *days and close friend):*

....

❛ *I and my husband, Richard, first met Lino and Augusta at The Westgate*
Hotel and like many of the Westgate regulars we then started coming to
The Butcher's Arms as soon as they moved there in 1973. Augusta was
famous in those early days for her ham and eggs, which was simply delicious.
A few weeks after our son, Charles, was born, we went to The Butcher's Arms
for dinner. It was our first night out after his birth and we arrived with the
baby in a carrycot. Augusta disappeared upstairs with him and we never saw
either of them again until about 11 pm when she came down and told us it was
time to go home because the baby needed feeding. Apparently she had sat
with him on the bed all evening.

Augusta and Lino love children and have that wonderful continental attitude
whereby children are always welcomed into their restaurant and made to feel
special. Of course, Lino is quite right when he says that they are the customers
of tomorrow. How true in our case. When our daughter, Emily, was seven years
old she was told she could go anywhere she wanted as a birthday treat.
We expected her to choose somewhere like McDonalds, but the only place she
wanted to go and celebrate was The Butcher's Arms! ❜

....

Eric Peres (Augusta's nephew):

....

❛ Augusta is a wonderful woman who wears her heart on her sleeve.

As well as being a very kind person, she is an exceptional cook.

I grew up with her in Paiágua and when she and Lino went to The Westgate

Hotel they got in touch to say that there would be a job there for me, too, if I

wanted it, so I left the village and went to join them. When they opened The

Butcher's Arms it was only natural that I should go with them. It was very

much an old fashioned pub when they first took over there, little more than a

stable. There is no doubt that Augusta's cooking and hard work played a big

part in helping to make the restaurant into the incredible success it is today.

She and Lino were like parents to me and the five years I spent working with

them were some of the best years of my life.

It has left me with wonderful memories.

I live back in Paiágua now, but I still get their

news and feel very close to them.

Despite being so many miles away,

I feel we still have the same relationship we

had when we started out together at

The Westgate all those years ago. ❜

....

Baroness Seccombe DBE (customer and friend for more than forty years):

....

❛ I first got to know Lino when he was working at
The Three Horseshoes in Rugby and then again at The
Westgate Hotel in Warwick, where we would often go for
lunch or dinner with my mother-in-law, Renee Seccombe.
It wasn't until we started going to The Butcher's Arms that
we became fully aware of Augusta. Little things like the
embroidered family tree on the wall of the restaurant, made
for her by a lady in the village, helped bring her to life.
My admiration for both Lino and Augusta then grew
steadily. I also recognised that neither of them could have
made the business into the success it is today on their own.
It took the two of them, and by working together with their
different strengths and qualities, they became the dream team.
Lino is the front man, while Augusta, far from being the grande dame, is the
quiet, practical, sensible one who is always working hard in the background,
helping the ship to sail firmly on. Her contribution to the fantastic success of the
restaurant has been invaluable. ❜

....

Margaret Hobbs (customer and close friend since 1973):

....

❛ Anybody who has been a customer of The Butcher's Arms since the very beginning, as I and my husband, David, have been, will be aware of Augusta's massive input into making the restaurant the success it is today. David and I would often be among the last to leave and I can still picture her coming out of the kitchen at the end of the evening with her apron on and no sooner had she taken it off and settled down for a chat than Lino would appear to announce that a late group had just arrived and he had told them: "Of course, no problem, Augusta will make you dinner." Augusta would simply smile, put the pinny on again and go back into the kitchen to make a wonderful dinner for another six or eight people, without a murmur.

To my mind she has always been Lino's wonderful secret weapon, the happy trouper who made all his promises work.

She would laugh and charm the customers, always concerned for their welfare and comfort, asking them: "Have you had enough? Did you enjoy that? Would you like some more?" ❜

Margaret Hobbs with Augusta and writer Michael Cable.

....

Peter Middleton (Former family doctor and friend):

· ·

❛ One Saturday morning in 1973, my wife Sue and I dropped into The Butcher's Arms after walking along the Oxford Canal below Priors Hardwick. Augusta asked us to stay behind after the rest of the customers had left the bar and we had lunch with her and Lino. The four of us struck up an immediate friendship that has endured through thick and thin.

In 1974 our first son, Edward, was born and Augusta insisted that we hold the christening lunch at The Butchers Arms. While Edward slept upstairs in her flat, our guests ate a splendid lunch prepared by Augusta.

Without Augusta there would simply be no business. It was her cooking that gave The Butcher's Arms its reputation in those early days. Lino is a magnificent presence front of house, but with the best will in the world, you wouldn't let him loose in the kitchen. Later, when they started employing a chef to help out, we used to make a point of dining there on his night off, just so that we could sample Augusta's wonderful cooking.

She has the extraordinary ability to make a meal out of anything. We were once staying with them in their villa in Portugal and there appeared to be little food in the house, but magically Augusta produced a delicious meal, seemingly out of nowhere. It was quite incredible.

On the surface, she may appear self absorbed and preoccupied with herself, but she is immensely strong, resolute and determined. I have nothing but admiration for the way

in which she has coped with the awful events of the last few years. Few people could have sustained what she has had to endure. She is a very emotional woman, in a Latin way, but that disguises her steely core. Against all the odds, she sails on regardless.

We are among the very few English friends who have visited the two neighbouring villages in Eastern Portugal where she and Lino were born. The contrast between her origins and her life now at The Butcher's Arms is striking. Starting with nothing, and without handouts, they worked tirelessly at whatever was demanded of them. From their early days as chambermaids in the Palacio do Seteais, they had quiet ambition. They observed how others lived and dreamt of better things. They learnt the art of personal service, the art of making each person feel special and important. So many people expect the good life with all the trimmings of affluence as a right. Lino and Augusta are different. They never expected to succeed without sheer hard work. Even now, if I ring up in the late afternoon, Augusta usually answers from the kitchen. Augusta is very intelligent and a shrewd judge of people. However, the quality I most associate with her is her generosity – not only generous of herself, but of anything that she has. She is unable to let you leave her house without giving you a present of something to eat – and that applies to everyone she knows. She is warm, kind, generous and very brave. I was her doctor for over 30 years and I have the greatest respect for her. I am honoured to be able to pay tribute to her. **❜**

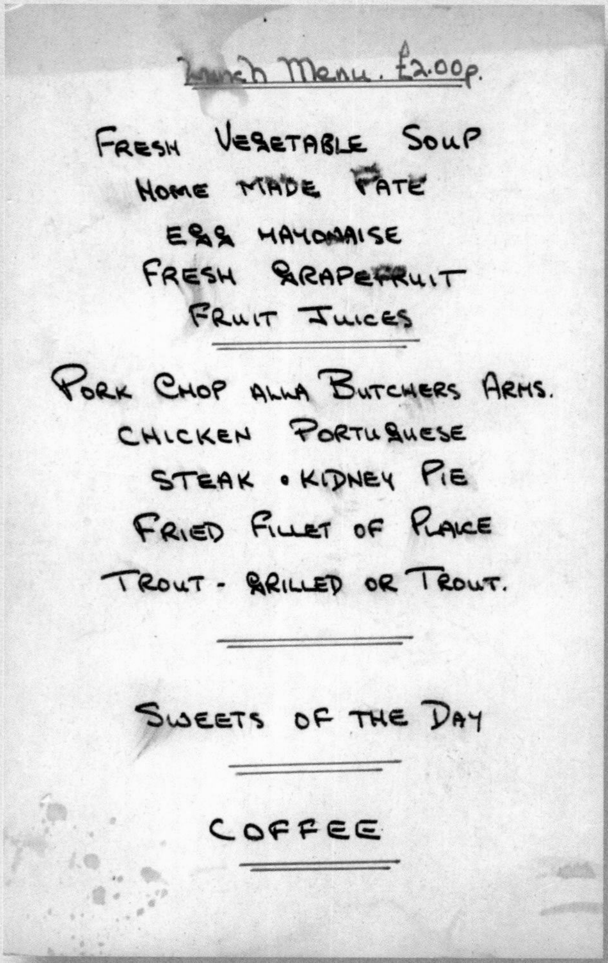

One of the early menus at The Butcher's Arms.

Chicken Liver Paté

This is one of the first recipes I made at The Butchers Arms. It is still as popular today as it was when it was offered on our lunch menu which cost just £2!

SERVES 10

4 oz/115g melted butter

1 lb/450g chicken livers

12 oz/350g diced belly of pork

1 egg

2 tablespoons red wine

2 tablespoons port

1 tablespoon brandy

salt and freshly ground black pepper

1 clove of garlic

bouquet garni (parsley, oregano, thyme, and one bay leaf
   bound together with string)

Melt the butter, add the pork, garlic, ground pepper and bouquet garni and cook until the pork is thoroughly cooked through. Add the chicken livers and continue for a further two minutes. The chicken livers will not look cooked at this stage.

Remove the bouquet garni and put the mixture, along with all the other ingredients, into a food processor or blender. Reduce to a puree. Pour the mixture into a foil lined 2 pint (1.2 litre) loaf tin or terrine. Cover with foil. Place in a small roasting tin, half filled with boiling water. Cook in a moderately hot oven for 1½ hours. The pate is cooked if the juices run clear when the centre is pierced with a skewer.

Remove the paté from the oven and leave to become quite cold before turning out onto a serving dish.

Kleftico
LAMB SHANKS

Along with many of our male customers, Tony Mason, the TV presenter and former rally driver, says this is his favourite dish. It is definitely hale and hearty. I use gravy in this recipe but you can substitute red wine or stock if you prefer although you will not get such a nice thick sauce.

SERVES 6

6 lamb shanks, trimmed	bay leaf
2 carrots, roughly chopped	parsley, chopped
1 onion	olive oil
2–3 cloves of garlic	tin of chopped tomatoes
2 sticks of celery	1 tablespoon tomato puree
1 leek, roughly chopped	salt and freshly ground black pepper
1 sprig of thyme	gravy (or 375 ml red wine)

Brown the lamb shanks in oil. In a separate, large casserole pot, sauté the onion, garlic, celery, carrot, leek and parsley and black pepper. When the ingredients have softened add the tomato pureé. Add the chopped tomatoes and gravy (or wine) and bring to the boil. When cooked, blitz all the ingredients in a blender or food processor and pour over the shanks. Add the bayleaf, sprig of thyme and salt. Place everything in a large roasting tin and cover with foil. Cook in the oven for approximately 1½–2 hours at 200 C, or until the lamb is falling off the bone.

Serve with mashed potatoes

Lemon Soufflé

When Lino and I lived in the house next door to The Butcher's Arms and we had visitors I would make this soufflé which is one of Marguerite Patten's recipes. It was quite time consuming but everybody loved it.

A 6 inch soufflé dish.

finely grated rind of two lemons
4 tablespoons/60ml lemon juice
3 eggs (separated)
4–6 oz/115-175g caster sugar
¾ tablespoon powdered gelatine

4 tablespoons/60 ml cold water
½ pint/300ml thick cream

TO DECORATE
small ratafia biscuits, crushed

Put the lemon rind, lemon juice, egg yolks and sugar into a basin. Place over a pan of very hot water. Whisk until thick and creamy.

Soften the gelatine in the cold water, add to the egg yolk mixture and continue to stir over the heat until the gelatine has dissolved. Cool and allow to stiffen slightly.

Whip the cream lightly and fold into the mixture. Whisk the egg whites until stiff, but not too dry and then fold into the mixture.

Cut a band of greaseproof paper, three times the depth of the soufflé dish. Fold the paper to give a double thickness and brush the part that will stand above the dish with a very light coating of melted butter. Tie or pin the band of paper very securely around the outside of the soufflé dish. Spoon the mixture into the dish.

Allow to set and then remove the paper slowly and carefully. Decorate the top and sides with the crushed ratafia biscuits

Tarte de Amendoa
ALMOND TART

This tart is absolutely gorgeous. It has a rich, buttery base, with a crunchy, nutty crust. It is so delicious that I had to stop making it for the dessert trolley because the staff would eat it all up, they couldn't resist it. I even made extra ones for them but they would eat those too. But do try it at home...

FOR THE BASE:

7 oz/200g self raising flour
3½ oz /100g margarine or butter
3½ oz/100g sugar
1 large egg, beaten
baking powder
pinch of salt

FOR THE FILLING:

4½ oz/120g sugar
3½ oz/100g butter
5½ oz/150g almonds (flaked)
5 dessertspoons milk (or cream)
drop of vanilla essence

To make the base
Cream together the butter and sugar. Sieve in the flour. Beat in the egg, salt and baking powder. Blend thoroughly. Spread it evenly over the base of a 9-inch well greased tart pan. Bake for about 20 minutes or until it is firm and lightly brown. Let it cool for about 15 minutes.

For the topping
In a small saucepan cook the sugar and butter over a low heat, stirring until the mixture turns light brown, making sure it doesn't burn. Slowly add the milk (or cream) and cook, stirring until the mixture is smooth. Stir in the almonds and continue to cook for a few more minutes.

Spread over the top of the cooled baked cake. Bake for another 20 minutes or so until the topping is bubbling and browned.

Tarte de Amêndoa

Para a massa do fundo: 200 g de farinha de trigo, 100 g de margarina, 100 g de açucar, 1 ovo, 0,5 dl de leite ou 5 colheres (sopa), 1 colher (chá) de fermento em pó, 1 pitadinha de sal.

Para o creme: 120 g de açucar; 100 g de margarina, 150 g de amêndoa (miolo), 1 pitada de baunilha ou açucar baunilhado. Necessária ainda: margarina para untar a forma da Tarte.

Para preparar a massa, deite os 200 g de farinha de trigo eo fermento numa tigela, abra uma cavidade no meio e aí amasse 1° o açucar com a margarina e depois com o ovo o leite e a pitadinha de sal. Envolva depois tudo com a farinha, formando massa como a de bolachas mas mais mole (procure não trabalhar muito a massa para que esta não ganhe elasticidade). Deixe repousar 15 a 20 minutos.

Entretanto, escalde as amêndoas retire-lhes a pele e corte-as em falhinhas.

Unte a forma com margarina e, mesmo com as pontas dos dedos, espalhe nela a massa de modo que nos bordos fique ligeiramente mais alta e pelo meio fique lisa e mais ou menos da mesma grossura, polvilhe-

com farinha para não se pegar aos

Augusta's Almond Tart recipe.

Part Seven

Homes and Gardens

It was as gardeners rather than restaurateurs that Augusta and Lino enjoyed their first taste of national TV exposure.

When the couple took over *The Butcher's Arms* in 1973 there was no flower-bedecked patio and no proper garden – just a rough paddock up at the back. However, within five years of their arrival the restaurant was doing so well that they felt they could afford to buy the two-bedroom cottage next door, which they then proceeded to do up and extend with a view to moving in and living there rather than 'over the shop'. The new property came with several acres of meadowland that adjoined their existing land and this gave them the idea of putting the two together and turning the combined area into a showpiece garden as an added attraction for their customers.

As this project progressed, it soon became clear that as well as her extraordinary talent for embroidery and crochet work Augusta was also blessed with green fingers. Lino, too, had become interested in gardening during his time at Claybrooke Grange and, of course, they had both had plenty of experience of working on the land during their early years in Paiágua and Vinha.

Inspired by visits to the open gardens at Hidcote and Kifsgate and by annual trips to the Chelsea Flower Show, they set out to create something on a fairly grand and ambitious scale. To help them achieve this, they first sought expert assistance from Valery Stevenson, a trained horticulturalist and professional garden designer living nearby in Priors Marston. After Valery had come up with the plans for the overall layout and also the positioning and shape of the various beds and the selection of flowers and shrubs that would be most suitable in each location, Augusta and Lino themselves then got down to the actual spadework involved in transforming the landscape architect's drawings into reality.

During the next couple of years they planted literally hundreds of trees, shrubs and flowers over a total area that amounted to more than four-and-a-half acres. Throughout that time, virtually every spare moment was devoted to the all-year-round task of tending to their increasingly spectacular creation. While Lino did the heavy digging, Augusta busied herself with the lighter, more cosmetic tasks – pruning, clipping, weeding and generally making sure that everything looked picture perfect. For her, especially, the many hours she spent out in the garden not only gave enormous pleasure and satisfaction but also provided a welcome and joyous relief from the otherwise relentless pressure of running the ever busier and more successful restaurant.

Once everything in the garden became established, the results were breathtaking. Throughout the spring and summer and into early autumn the beds would be ablaze with colour. As well as the massed ranks of begonias, peonies, pansies, delphiniums and all the usual cottage garden favourites, there were azaleas and roses of every kind, rare ornamental fruit trees and a wide variety of highly-scented flowering shrubs. And at the heart of it all was a large lake, with a waterfall and a rustic bridge from which giant Koi carp could be glimpsed gliding serenely beneath tiger lily pads.

(Top) The garden at The Butcher's Arms at the time it featured on BBC TV's Gardeners' World and (bottom) Augusta with grand-daughter Heather on the patio at The Butcher's Arms.

The cliff top view from above Praia Grande in Portugal,
where Augusta and Lino have a villa.

As had been hoped, customers fell in love with the garden, wandering around with their pre-dinner drinks or taking a twilight stroll after their meal on warm midsummer evenings. Lord Heseltine, a regular at *The Butcher's Arms* during his days as a Cabinet minister, was so impressed that he invited Augusta and Lino to go and have a look around the arboretum that he was in the process of creating at Thenford, his country home just a few miles away. Jack Profumo, another ex-Cabinet Minister who became a regular while living nearby and who was an extremely enthusiastic gardener himself, not only gave them useful tips but also presented Augusta with a climbing Wedding Rose that he had created. This was planted near the front entrance to the restaurant, where it continues to flourish, its pale yellow blooms smothering part of the wall from June onwards.

By 1990, the garden had become such a well-known and much talked about attraction in the area that it was featured on BBC TV's *Gardener's World*. Presenter Stefan Buczacki had been alerted to its existence by BBC colleague and *Butcher's Arms* regular Tony Mason, the former *Top Gear* star. Stefan and his team spent an entire day filming the half-hour special, which included interviews with Augusta and Lino. Augusta was thrilled to bits to hear one of the country's leading gardening experts marvelling at the way in which they had managed to transform a few acres of rough pasture into something so special. Following this TV exposure, it was also opened to the public as part of the National Gardens Scheme and, altogether, raised £60,000 for charity.

As time went by and the garden reached full maturity, the job of maintaining it properly and keeping everything looking immaculate became too much for Augusta and Lino, even with the help of a near full-time gardener, and so they reluctantly came to the conclusion that they would have to give it up. This coincided with their decision to sell the house next door. Although they had extended the original two-bedroom cottage into a handsome four-bedroom house, complete with an indoor swimming pool, they had never moved in. They were perfectly comfortable in the rooms above the restaurant, which they found were actually more convenient in practice. When they eventually sold the house to John Allen in 1995, the garden went with it. To Augusta's and Lino's great delight, John has continued to look after the garden as meticulously and as enthusiastically as they always did. "I was very careful to choose a good neighbour," says Lino.

Although sad to lose the wonderful showpiece that she and Lino had created out of nothing and had then tended with such pride and pleasure for more than seventeen years, Augusta by this time had other, more pressing priorities. Most importantly, the grandchildren had started to arrive and she wanted to spend as much of her spare time as possible with them rather than being a slave to the hoe, the rake and the secateurs. Apart from that, she and Lino now had acquired a villa in Portugal with a large garden that provided her with plenty of opportunity to exercise those green fingers of hers.

Just down the coast from Lisbon, the villa is located in a prime position high above Praia Grande, the beach where Augusta and Lino used to spend their afternoons off during their time in Sintra all those years ago. Facing due west, with a balcony that provides glorious and uninterrupted views of the sun setting over the sea, the property came with several acres of rough ground that Augusta once again set about transforming from a wilderness into a delightful garden. Here it is bougainvillea, bird of paradise lilies and frangipani that provide the colour rather than begonias, delphiniums and hollyhocks.

The villa in Portugal, another opportunity for
Augusta to show off her green-fingered talents and
(inset) Augusta and Lino outside the new house Lino
bought for his parents before he left Vinha.

Dining al fresco with family and friends in Portugal (main picture). (Top left) Augusta with sister Maria Santos in the garden of the villa at Colares and (bottom right) Lino outside Augusta's family home in Paiágua.

The villa is where she goes to get away from it all. When she and Lino fly in to Lisbon, they are often picked up by their old friend António 'Tony' Reis, the very same Seteais driver who took them down to the quayside on the day they left for England back in 1960, another nostalgic link with the past.

It is a two or three hour journey by car from Colares back up to Paiágua, but Augusta regularly makes the trip whenever she's in Portugal in order to visit her two surviving sisters, Maria Marques and Maria Santos, and her nephews Eric and José, the sons of Maria Marques. After working at *The Butcher's Arms* for many years before going to France to open a restaurant there with his brother José, Eric returned to the village, mainly to be near his mother in her old age but partly because his own sense of nostalgia drew him back. José, who worked with Lino at the Seteais and then later spent many years as head waiter at *The Butcher's Arms*, has also retired back to Paiágua. The two Marias never left and Maria Santos still lives in the house built by their father on the site of the barn where the animals used to be kept and where Augusta and Lino held their wedding reception.

Augusta treasures her childhood memories of how things used to be, but she has no great desire herself to try and turn the clock back by buying a holiday home there, even though an old traditional village house could be picked up for next to nothing now that so many people have moved away to the towns and cities. She has taken the grandchildren back on several occasions so that they will have an understanding of their roots. The tears well up in her eyes when she sees the old familiar landmarks – the house where she grew up, now derelict; the schoolhouse, no longer in use for that purpose now that there are virtually no young families living permanently in the village and no children to be taught; the communal oven, long abandoned and half-hidden behind weeds and rubbish; the dusty village square where she used to dance on fiesta days, once the heart of the community but now strangely quiet; the rickety extension to Lino's parents' home in Vinha in which she began her married life. All these things have enormous sentimental value, but they are part of another lifetime. She will never completely sever her connections with the place that has such a very special place in her heart. But Priors Hardwick will always be her home now. That is where the closest members of her family are and they are what matter most to her.

It is a measure of just how far Augusta has come in her extraordinary life's journey that the little barefoot girl who carried water from the well in a pitcher balanced on her head should have ended up going shopping in a Porsche; that a child who grew up living on cabbage soup should find herself winning plaudits from discerning diners for the quality of her gourmet food; and that someone whose mother could neither read nor write should see her own son and her grandchildren educated at some of the country's top public schools.

As she grew up eating all her meals from the same cracked earthenware bowl, she herself could never have imagined that she would one day be able to dine off exactly the same sort of plates as the Queen of England! Augusta never forgot the beautiful Royal Crown Derby bone china dinner service used by Mrs. Tahany at Claybrooke Grange and when she spotted the same service in a Warwick china shop shortly after she and Lino moved to Priors Hardwick, she was determined to buy it. To Augusta, owning that beautiful bone china symbolised the success that she and Lino had made of their lives

Augusta's collection of porcelain and bone china is a source of both pride and pleasure.

together. And, when shortly afterwards, she happened to see the Queen on television, drinking tea from a cup and saucer identical to the ones she herself now uses, she found herself almost bursting with pride.

Since then, her dining room above *The Butcher's Arms* has gradually been filled with exquisite Dresden porcelain figurines, flower vases and Royal Worcester bone china dinner and tea services – many of them just like those she had seen displayed at the Tahany's home. Augusta always thought they looked stunning and still gets enormous pleasure from being surrounded by such fine objects.

At the same time, she has never lost touch with the very different world in which she grew up. This is most graphically illustrated in the special little room upstairs at *The Butcher's Arms* where she has got a traditional-style loom set up. It was built for her by António Dias, a village craftsman from Paiágua who then came all the way to Priors Hardwick to install it for her, the first time in his life that the old man had ever been outside Portugal.

On this loom, which is exactly like the one on which she learned to weave as a girl, she continues to produce the raw material out of which she makes linen tablecloths, bedspreads, napkins and place mats, all decorated with the most intricate and delicate embroidery and lace crochet work. This is her favourite form of relaxation and whenever she has a spare moment or two she retires to her little workroom and either sits down at the loom or picks up her needles to continue working on her latest piece. Even when she is watching television, her needles will be endlessly clicking away, producing another masterpiece with apparently effortless skill.

She often has to smile and shake her head in disbelief when she recalls how, as a girl, she used to walk miles to buy her yarn and thread from a little shop in the next village to Paiágua. Today, the only way she can get hold of the special yarn needed for her crochet work is through the Internet.

She has drawers filled with the most beautiful examples of her work, going all the way back to the very first piece of embroidery that she ever did. She was only fourteen at the time and the pretty flower design actually got her into trouble when it emerged that she had used a 200-year-old piece of linen belonging to her grandmother.

Nobody who sees her extraordinary collection, which includes large tablecloths and vast

The most intricate and delicate embroidery and lace crochet work.

double bedspreads, can fail to be impressed by the sheer quality of her craftsmanship. It is simply breathtaking. At the famous charity auction organised in aid of the Royal Marsden Hospital in 1998 and attended by a glittering array of VIPs and local Midlands personalities, it was one of her tablecloths that attracted some of the keenest bidding of the whole evening, eventually fetching £1,200.

An equally splendid table top runner was given as a present to Professor David Cunningham, the cancer specialist at the Royal Marsden who has treated both Augusta and her son, Peter. Having already been presented with a cheque for £82,500 for his Research Fund as a result of the charity auction, Dr Cunningham was quite overwhelmed by this further, very personal gesture from a mother whose gratitude to him for saving her son's life knew no bounds.

Many others have benefited from Augusta's warm-hearted generosity of spirit, purely out of friendship. It is the quality remarked upon by all who know her well. And Lino is the same. Talk to their friends – and virtually every regular customer comes to be regarded as a close personal friend – and you will hear nothing but stories of gifts and treats freely dispensed, small kindnesses endlessly done, help and support offered in times of crisis and calls made at times of difficulty "just to make sure everything is all right". There can't be many restaurateurs who get on so well with their customers that they end up going on holiday with them, inviting them to their villa, taking them out to lunch and, in Augusta's case, even babysitting their children from time to time so that they can enjoy a quiet meal together!

These are the things that help to make them such a very special couple.

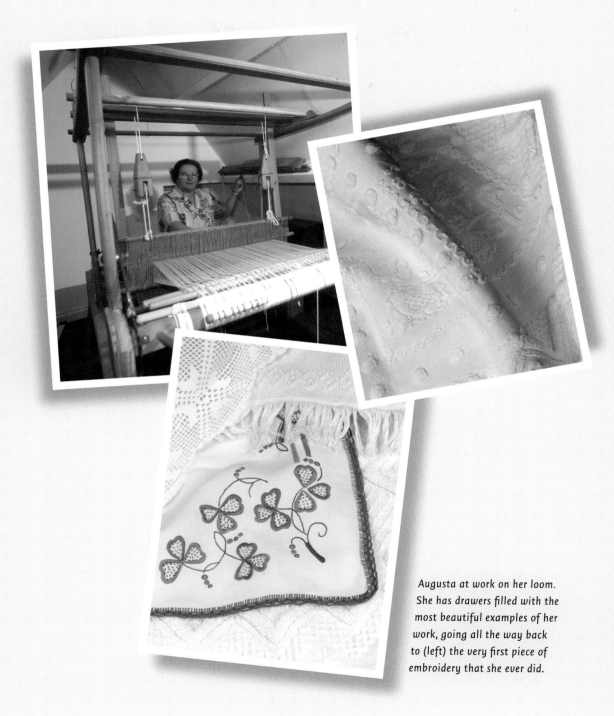

Augusta at work on her loom. She has drawers filled with the most beautiful examples of her work, going all the way back to (left) the very first piece of embroidery that she ever did.

Judith Pearson (right, with husband Tim and Augusta and Leno in The Rockies):

....

❛ My husband Tim and I shared many holidays with Augusta and Lino,
including trips to The Rockies in Canada and Florida. During our visit to
Disneyworld Augusta fell in love again. Meals in our hotel were always
enlivened by Disney characters walking around, signing autographs, fooling
about and giving people a hug. Augusta was completely into it. She really let
herself believe in these characters, and it was Goofy she loved most of all.
She absolutely adored him and so now, whenever I go to Florida, I send her
a postcard, telling her that Goofy asked after her and sends his love. ❜

....

Sylvia Sutherland (friend and neighbour, pictured in white, below):

. . . .

' For many years now a large group of us have gone carol singing in the village on Christmas Eve, ending up at The Butcher's Arms, where we are always warmly welcomed and invited into the dining room to sing for the customers. Augusta loves this annual event and always gets very emotional, especially when we sing 'Silent Night', her favourite carol. Recently, when she was ill and confined to bed upstairs, we sang it underneath her bedroom window. She and Lino – and all the diners – always give very generously to whichever charity we are collecting for. Afterwards we are taken into the lounge bar and given as much wine as we can drink. '

. . . .

Tony Mason (TV presenter and former RAC Rally winner):
....

'Obviously much of my interest centres around cars and I have spent hours chatting about them to Lino and Peter as well as visiting The Butcher's Arms with various top motorsport drivers. However, I seldom thought to talk about cars when chatting to Augusta and so it was some time before I discovered that she was the proud owner of a Porsche.

Augusta loves this car and has owned it from new. It currently has 60,000 miles on the clock, most of which have been incurred on regular trips to nearby Southam and Leamington Spa to purchase flowers and other items for The Butchers Arms as well as for visits to hair salons and dress shops!

Augusta enthuses about her Porsche and is no doubt a very good driver. However, it is as back seat driver that she really comes into her own. If there was motorsport category for back seat driving, Augusta would be world champion. I once accompanied Lino and Augusta to check out a new restaurant that had opened in deepest Warwickshire and to meet up with their long-time friends and customers, Harry and Peggy Webster. We were in a new Range Rover that was on loan to Lino. I was in the front with Lino and while Augusta was perched on the edge of the rear seat holding onto the front seats, one in each hand. Lino and I were pretty certain of the route, but Augusta was hilarious, issuing instructions about which turn to take or ignore and constantly reprimanding Lino on his every move. She seemed convinced that he was totally unfamiliar with the controls of the Range Rover, although he was driving superbly. Augusta's generosity is renowned of course, but she does things very subtly. I remember visiting The Butchers Arms late one Sunday morning to give Lino a message and briefly to talk about some filming that I was planning to do at the restaurant with the BBC. I was in a hurry as I had to return home for gardening duties, but somehow Augusta picked up on the fact that my wife was away and without a word being said I was quickly handed a magnificent roast beef Sunday lunch with all the trimmings. The plate was neatly wrapped in tinfoil to retain the heat and I was sent on my merry way clutching what was, without doubt, the best "take-away" that I have ever had. **)**

....

Professor Stefan Buczacki

. . . .

'In the course of several decades of covering gardens for the broadcasting media, there are relatively few that are stamped truly indelibly in the memory. The Butcher's Arms is one. In part this is because a visit to the garden was one of the first pieces I recorded for Gardeners' World on BBC2. But above all, it is in my memory for its beautiful planting, its imaginative design, for Lino and for Augusta, who was subjected to repeated demands on her presentational skills and came through it all smiling and as cheerful as she always is. It was only later, as I sat in the restaurant and, through the windows of the conservatory, admired some of the most magnificent cymbidium orchids and brugmansias (better known I am sure to most customers as daturas or simply angel's trumpets) that I have ever seen that I realised Augusta was not just a pretty face smiling among the herbage but was a woman possessed of

quite extraordinary and special horticultural skill. Although the great garden is now owned by their neighbour, it is hugely gratifying and reassuring to see that at The Butcher's Arms today, nothing else has changed. Augusta's smile and her plants are as magnificent and welcoming as ever.'

. . . .

Andreas Antona (chef patron of Simpsons Restaurant, Edgebaston, Birmingham):

. . . .

‘ Portugal is a macho male society and Lino embodies that, but like all good

Portuguese families the heart of the matter rests with the mother. Augusta,

being a true matriarch, is the engine driving the whole thing – and doing it

in such a quiet way that Lino's nose is not put out of joint.

Augusta and Lino have had an incredible journey in life and their achievements

are simply amazing. My parents came from a similar background so I can truly

appreciate how hard they have worked to become the success they are today.

And as a fellow restaurateur and a customer of The Butcher's Arms for over

20 years, I am full of admiration for what they have achieved. Fads in cuisine

come and go but Augusta and Lino have stuck to their guns and have never

produced anything less than the highest standard in service, food and wine.

And to a large extent that is down to Augusta's eye for detail,

determination and her sheer love for the job. ’

. . . .

Margo Salt (customer and friend):

....

❛ My husband Derek and I have enjoyed many holidays and fun times together –
in Switzerland, in South Africa and at their beautiful villa in Portugal. During
our South African trip we were all travelling up Table Mountain in a cable car
when Lino said jokingly: "This would be a good place to push off the wife!"
Augusta was shocked, but she had the last laugh because when we reached the
summit Lino tried to feed one of the dassies, the rock rabbits that live on the
mountain, and it almost bit his finger off. Augusta cried tears of laughter –
she thought it was hilarious.

I've always been struck by her tremendous love of flowers. Wherever we went in
the world, the first things Augusta wanted to see were the local gardens and
parks. She clearly found them wonderfully relaxing and uplifting. Plants and
flowers mean a lot to her – particularly roses, which she adores.

That love of flowers also explains why she can produce such wonderful
arrangements for the restaurant. They are the first things you see when you
enter The Butcher's Arms and they are always beautifully done. ❜

....

Augusta and Lino with Derek Salt during a holiday in South Africa.
(Inset) Margo Salt with Lino.

Valery Stephenson (Garden Designer):

....

❛ Augusta is a natural gardener – and a very tidy one, unlike Lino!
She loves plants and flowers and adored the garden that she worked so hard
to perfect. Being in the garden clearly gave her enormous pleasure and she
found it very relaxing.

She and Lino would visit places such as Kifsgate Gardens and Hidcote Manor
Gardens to get ideas. And then early each morning she would be out in the
garden, weeding, planting, pruning while Lino did a lot of the hard work,
such as the digging.

Her delphiniums and roses were superb and when she discovered that
rhododendrons, which she loved, were unsuited to the Priors Hardwick soil,
she refused to give up and simply placed them in pots, ending up with
a wonderful display that gave pleasure not only to her but to all
The Butcher's Arms customers as well. ❜

....

Margaret Clarke (neighbour and friend):

....

❛ Augusta and I both enjoy walking in the countryside around Priors Hardwick
and there is one particularly pleasant footpath through the fields behind
The Butcher's Arms. Unfortunately, the walk is possibly a bit longer than
some of us would wish to go. I had spied that there was an opportunity for a
shortcut, although it meant crawling through a hole in the hedge, made by
badgers. You had to duck under the wire, go down into the ditch and up over the
other side. It was some time later, talking to Augusta one day, that I discovered
that both of us were secretly sneaking through the same hole to cut short our
walk and avoid going up a steep hill.

What I really adore is Augusta's kindness. Both she and Lino are so thoughtful.
The first year after I was widowed, I met Augusta a week before Christmas and
she asked me what I was doing on Christmas Day. I told her I had been invited
to lunch by the vicar. She obviously went straight home and told Lino.
At 8 o'clock on Christmas morning Lino arrived on my doorstep with a big
basket of chocolates and four bottles of wine to take to lunch at the vicarage.
It was such a kind gesture — I was completely overcome. ❜

....

Fenella Gent (Augusta's hairdresser):

....

'I've been Augusta's hairdresser on and off for almost thirty years. Her regular Friday morning sessions are her little treat. She has an overwhelming generosity of spirit and is so open-hearted to everybody. She always arrives with some food – salmon, profiteroles, wine or champagne – and always four custard tarts from Marks and Spencer, because she knows how much I love them.

Whatever is going on in her life, she always shares it with us, but most of the time she is more concerned about other people in the salon – the hairdressers and the other regular customers.

When she first bought her Porsche, she came in and was really excited about it. In her usual modest way, she said that nobody would expect a woman like her

to get out of such a fancy car. So, we all had a laugh the day she returned to the car and discovered a note on the windscreen from a complete stranger who was obviously very taken with the thought of such a powerful car being driven by a woman and left his phone number, saying he would love to meet her. The note was quite suggestive, which really amused Augusta. She still talks about it. '

....

John Allen (friend and neighbour):

. . . .

A – *is for 'amazing', which is what Augusta is. She has a wonderful inner strength that never fails to shine through, and in the face of adversity, she is very stoic. Along with those qualities, Augusta has a very mischievous sense of humour!!!*

U – *is for her totally 'unselfish' nature. She always worries more about how everyone else is rather than thinking about herself.*

G – *is for her 'genuine' depth of caring, not only her family, but also for friends and customers alike.*

U – *is for 'us' and our friendship. We have known Augusta and Lino for many years, and have become very good friends since moving in next door!!!!*

S – *is for 'sleeve'. Because with Augusta, that is where she wears her heart.*

T – *is for 'tears'. Augusta cries when she is happy as well as when she is sad, so there have many tears shed over the years one way or another!!*

A – *is for 'always'. Augusta, Lino and The Butchers Arms, hold so many 'memories', not only for Jan & I, my children and grand children, but also for so many other families who have been frequenting the 'Butcher's' for well over thirty years and experiencing the very special ambience it holds. This has been made possible through Augusta being prepared to put 120% into the business, all day and everyday. Augusta has never forgotten her roots, and because of that, The Butcher's is where it is today, in the heart of many of its customers. It is the place to go for special occasions. The 'memories' are irreplaceable.*

. . . .

Mushroom and Stilton Tart

SERVES 4

8 oz/225g shortcrust pastry

5½ oz/150g Stilton cheese, grated

3½ oz/100g field mushrooms

1 onion, finely chopped

olive oil

fresh coriander

1 teaspoon coriander powder

3 eggs

8 fl oz/225 ml double cream

salt and freshly ground black pepper

nutmeg

Line a quiche or flan dish with the pastry and place in the refrigerator to chill. Slice the mushrooms and sauté them together with the finely chopped onion in a tablespoonful of olive oil. Season with some freshly chopped coriander, coriander powder, salt and pepper. Place in a colander and drain off any excess fluid and put the mixture into the pastry case. Top with the grated Stilton cheese. Beat the eggs and cream together with a little black pepper and the grated nutmeg and pour over the tart mixture, making sure it covers the cheese. Place on a baking tray and cook in a pre-heated medium hot oven until it is golden brown. Before taking out of the oven, gently agitate the tray to check that the mixture is firm and therefore cooked. (I call this the 'wobble' test). This is equally delicious eaten hot or cold.

Steak Diane

This is not a Portuguese recipe of course. But when we introduced it into The Butcher's Arms menu it became very popular. The dish originated at the Savoy Hotel, in London in 1954 and we first came across it when it was served at The Three Horseshoes in Rugby where we used to work.

When Italian cooking became fashionable everybody started cooking a thin steak at the table, with mushrooms and cream. But my boss at The Three Horseshoes refused to do it differently – and we still prefer to do it the classic way here at The Butcher's Arms.

I taught the celebrity chef Tony Tobin, who started his career as a kitchen hand with us, how to cook Steak Diane and now he does it on TV – it's even on the BBC website.

We always cook this at the table and flambé it with a dash of brandy. Of course that does produce an enormous flame because people like a little bit of a show – but if you are cooking this at home it would be safer to use the ingredient that Tony Tobin has substituted – balsamic vinegar.

SERVES 1

½ rump steak or a fillet steak

2 tablespoons olive oil

½ onion, peeled and diced

splash of Worcestershire sauce

1 teaspoon wholegrain mustard

drizzle of olive oil

drizzle of balsamic vinegar – or brandy

Heat the oil in a pan and sauté the onion for 5–6 minutes until lightly browned.

Push the onion to one side and stir in the Worcestershire sauce, mustard, drizzle of oil and balsamic vinegar and simmer for a few minutes.

Bash out the steak using a meat mallet so that it becomes quite thin. Pan fry the steak for around 3 minutes on each side, or according to personal taste.

Strawberry Cheesecake

FOR THE BASE

1 packet digestive biscuits

4½ oz/125 g butter

FILLING

18 fl oz/500 ml double cream

14 oz/40 g Philadelphia cream cheese

10½ oz/300 g caster sugar

7 fl oz/200 ml strawberry juice

vanilla pod

vanilla essence

5 leaves gelatine

Crush up the biscuits. Melt the butter and add to the biscuits. Press into the bottom of a cake tin and place in a refrigerator to chill. Heat up the strawberry juice in a pan and add the softened gelatine until dissolved. Put in a food mixer, together with the inside of the vanilla pod, the essence and sugar. Whisk until it looks like meringue. Add the cheese first, mix again and then add the cream and mix until thick.

Pour onto the chilled biscuit base. Chill again before serving.

Chocolate Profiteroles

Choux pastry is the lightest, crispiest, airiest pastry. I learned to make it when we moved to England and I've since taught some our chefs at The Butcher's Arms how to make it. What is really good about choux is that it doesn't call for any particular pastry skills like lightness of hand or careful rolling.

MAKES 20 CHOUX BUNS

FOR THE CHOUX PASTRY

7 fl oz/200ml cold water

½ teaspoon caster sugar

3 oz/85g unsalted butter

pinch salt

4 oz/115g plain flour

4 medium eggs ,beaten

FOR THE CREAM FILLING

1 pint/600ml double cream

½ oz/15g or 1 tablespoon icing sugar

FOR THE CHOCOLATE SAUCE

½ oz/15g butter

4 tablespoons/60ml water

6 oz/175g good quality plain chocolate, broken into pieces

Preheat the oven to 200C//400F/Gas 6

To make the pastry, place the butter, water and sugar into a large saucepan.
Place over a low heat to melt the butter. Increase the heat and shoot in the flour and salt

in one go. Remove from the heat and quickly beat the mixture vigorously until a smooth paste is formed, stirring continuously to dry out the paste.

Once the paste curls away from the side of the pan, transfer the mixture into a large bowl and leave to cool for 10–15 minutes.

Beat in the eggs, a little at a time, stirring hard until the paste is smooth and glossy. Continue adding the egg until you have a smooth dropping consistency. It may not be necessary to add all the egg. The mixture will be shiny and smooth and will fall reluctantly from a spoon if it is given a sharp jerk.

Lightly oil a large baking tray. Using a piping bag, pipe the mixture into 'blobs' onto the tray. Bake for 25–30 minutes, until golden brown. If too pale they will become soggy when cool.

Remove from the oven and prick the base of each profiterole. Place onto the baking tray with the hole facing upwards and return to the oven for 5 minutes. The warm air from the oven helps to dry the middle of the profiteroles.

Prepare the filling. Lightly whip the cream and icing sugar until soft peaks form. Do not overwhip.When the profiteroles are cold, using a piping bag with a plain nozzle, pipe the cream into the holes of the profiteroles. If a piping bag is not available cut the profiteroles in half and spoon in the cream with a teaspoon.

Prepare the chocolate sauce. Melt the chocolate with the water and butter in a bowl placed over a saucepan of boiling water. Stir without boiling until smooth and shiny. Arrange the buns on a serving dish and pour over the sauce. Eat cold.

A look of sheer delight.

Part Eight

Family Values

EVERY PICTURE TELLS A STORY — AND THERE IS
A PARTICULAR SHOT OF AUGUSTA, TAKEN ON
AUGUST 15TH, 1989, THAT LEAVES NO DOUBT
THAT THIS WAS ONE OF THE HAPPIEST DAYS OF
HER LIFE.

The look on her face is one of sheer delight – and the reason? Son Peter was getting married
to Helen, the beautiful, spirited girl who had won Augusta's heart as well as Peter's.

The couple first met when Peter and some of his mates gatecrashed Helen's 18th
birthday party at the village hall in Staverton, just down the road from Priors Hardwick.
Helen immediately caught Peter's eye and he managed to engineer an apparently accidental
meeting a few days later at which point he invited her to a friend's posh 21st at Hambleton
Hall. From then on, the two of them were inseparable and both Augusta and Lino were
overjoyed when, after a five-year courtship, they decided to go ahead and get married.

"We are so lucky to have such a wonderful daughter-in-law," says Augusta.
"In fact, we don't think of her as a daughter-in-law, but simply as our daughter. She has
made Peter very happy and together, they have given me three wonderful grandchildren.
What more could I ask?"

The wedding took place in Southam's Roman Catholic church and was followed by
a reception at *The Butcher's Arms* – the only time since Lino and Augusta have been there that

the restaurant has ever been closed all day. Twenty-five members of Lino's and Augusta's families came over from Portugal, along with the accordionist from Paiágua who used to play for them in the village square all those years ago, while a contingent from one side of Helen's family flew in from Dublin. With the happy couple arriving at the reception in style in a vintage Le Mans Bentley loaned by a *Butcher's Arms* regular, Reg Parker, it was a very colourful and lively international affair. After the honeymoon, the new Mr and Mrs Pires settled into a small two-bedroom cottage in the village.

Peter had already joined the family business by this time and was helping his parents to run the restaurant – much to Augusta's delight. For someone whose natural maternal instincts have always been so strong and for whom family is all important, it was a huge bonus to be able to have her son living and working in such close proximity, even more so once the grandchildren started arriving. It is as 'Nanny' to Heather, Edward and James that Augusta is really in her element.

All three were born in the month of May, as was Lino, so May is definitely party time in the Pires household. And all three youngsters have very distinct personalities. Heather, the eldest, has always been very grown-up for her age. Very bright and extremely literate, she started writing poems and stories from a very early age to mark family events and followed her father to Rugby School at eleven. One of a small minority of girls at the school, it was Heather herself who insisted on going there. Edward is very like Lino, boisterous, extrovert, full of fun and mischief, while James, the youngest, is like a miniature version of Peter, quieter and more serious. Needless to say, they are all spoiled rotten by Augusta.

Thirteeen years ago Peter moved from the cottage into Manor Farm, directly behind

Lino and Augusta with Peter and Helen on their wedding day.

The grandchildren.
(Top left, l to r) Edward,
Heather and James, (Top right)
Heather, (Bottom) Augusta and
Lino with (l to r) James, Heather
and Edward.

The Butcher's Arms, and having him and the family all within such easy reach is a great blessing for Augusta. The time she is able to spend with them helps to make up for the years when Peter was growing up and she fretted about the fact that pressure of work prevented her from being quite as much of a full-time mum as she would have liked. She found it extremely difficult when, shortly after the move to *The Butcher's Arms* in 1973, Peter had to start boarding at Emscote Lawn. There was no real alternative because, with Augusta and Lino both busy in the restaurant from 6.00pm onwards, Peter, who was then nine, often had to be left on his own upstairs to do his homework and look after himself. Augusta was desperately upset when it was decided that boarding was the only answer and she would find any excuse to go to Leamington so that she could pop in and visit him at the school with sweets and other treats.

She found it even harder when Peter then moved on from Emscote Lawn to Rugby. It was a proud day for both Lino and Augusta when they dropped him off there with his trunk and his tuck box to start his first term, but Augusta cried all the way home. They had always rather hoped that he would follow in their footsteps when it came to choosing a career and with this in mind Lino had taken the precaution of putting his name down well in advance for *L'Ecole Hôtelière de Lausanne*, Europe's No 1 catering college. Peter did briefly consider going on to university to do law or economics. With his lifelong love of high performance cars, he was also tempted towards the motor industry and the idea of one day opening a garage or dealership of his own. Happily, however, he decided in the end that the restaurant business offered him a more secure future and, in 1983, he duly took up his place at Lausanne.

*Family tree, embroidered for Augusta
by a friend in Priors Hardwick.*

After just one year of the intensive four-year course, all of which was conducted entirely in French, he then came to the conclusion that he was wasting his time. The formal qualification would certainly have been invaluable if he were planning to make his own way in the hotel business, a passport to a top job anywhere in the world. But once he had made up his mind to carry on the increasingly successful family business there seemed no point in spending three more expensive years being taught things that he could learn just as well through working alongside his parents.

They have been operating together as a team since 1984 and, having started at the bottom as a barman and waiter, Peter has gradually taken over all the daily administrative side of the business as well as sharing the front-of house duties with Lino. Fathers and sons often find that working closely together can be difficult and in an environment as notoriously volatile as the restaurant business, where the traditional behind-the-scenes image is of temperamental chefs and harassed staff struggling to keep their cool in the pressure cooker atmosphere of a busy, peak-time kitchen, you would think that such family relationships would be strained to the limit. And yet Lino and Peter, although they may not see eye-to-eye on everything, have rarely had a serious difference of opinion over the last twenty-three years. The secret, they say, is that they each have their own areas of responsibility and get on with the job without trying to tell each other what to do. While Lino is more than happy to leave all the paperwork to Peter, Peter is content to let Lino be the star. And Augusta prefers to remain in the background, quietly making sure that everything keeps running smoothly.

The strength of the bonds that hold the family together has been clearly demonstrated in recent years by the manner in which they have coped with a series of major health crises, each of them sudden, unexpected and potentially devastating. What is so remarkable about the way they dealt with these situations is that, despite the fact that they must have found them physically, mentally and emotionally draining, they not only kept each other going but somehow managed to keep the business running normally at the same time.

First to suffer was Peter, diagnosed with cancer in 1997. For several weeks his life hung in the balance, and he was only saved in the end by the skill and dedication of Professor David Cunningham and his team at the Royal Marsden Hospital. Peter was in and out of the hospital for four months altogether and underwent six separate courses of chemotherapy. During those first few weeks when he never left his bed at the Royal Marsden, Helen and Augusta moved into family accommodation at the hospital so that one or other of them could be at his bedside round the clock. Lino travelled up to Sutton, Surrey every morning to visit before returning to Priors Hardwick in time to open the restaurant for lunch.

Regular customers rallied round to provide a fantastic support system, not only doing their best to boost morale and provide shoulders to cry on, but also offering practical help in the form of lifts to and from the hospital. And when Peter had finally been given the all-clear and Lino and Augusta organised a special charity auction dinner at the restaurant to raise money for Professor Cunningham's research fund as a mark of gratitude for what he and his team had done, those same customers responded by bidding an incredible total of £82,500 for the thirty-six items that were auctioned, another indication of the tremendous affection with which the family is regarded.

For Augusta, the months of worry and the long vigil at the hospital, when it was still very much touch and go, amounted to the most terrible ordeal, a time of sleepless nights and moments of the deepest despair. And yet beneath that shy, self-effacing exterior and apparently fragile self-confidence, she possesses hidden reserves of quiet inner strength. This was clearly demonstrated six years later when, by some cruel and coincidental stroke of fate, she herself was diagnosed with cancer.

Once again, Professor Cunningham came to the rescue, ensuring that she had the best possible care. Her treatment included two major operations and a course of chemotherapy that involved week-long stays at the Royal Marsden's Fulham Road hospital. In the middle of all this, Peter had a bad fall and cracked a rib, leading to a severe lung infection that laid him low for a while. And, as if that were not enough, Lino then developed medical problems that required him to be admitted to the John Radcliffe hospital in Oxford for a series of tests and, eventually, an operation. At one point, both he and Augusta were in different hospital beds at the same time – Augusta in London and Lino in Oxford – talking to each other on their mobile phones.

Such a relentless succession of blows might have floored a lesser person completely. Augusta, however, although understandably tearful at times, reacted generally with a calm fortitude and, true to character, seemed far more concerned about Peter and

Lino than she was about herself. And as soon as she was reasonably fit again, she was back on duty, helping them out in the restaurant as usual. Amazingly, the busy routine there had carried on throughout this critical period as if nothing particularly untoward were going on behind the scenes. Like the showman he is, Lino allows virtually nothing to prevent him from donning his blazer and sprucing himself up every morning at around noon and every evening at 6.oopm, ready to start greeting another full house of customers. But as he admits, there have been times over the last few years when he has been reminded of that line from a song that goes: "Smile though your heart is aching..."

For Augusta, as for Lino, *The Butcher's Arms* is not so much a thriving business, more a way of life. Their entire daily routine continues to revolve around it from the moment they get up in the morning to the minute they go to bed at night after the last customer has left. It is where they see all their best friends on a regular basis, the distinction between old friends and regular customers often blurred. That is why they find it so hard to contemplate the idea of retirement, even of slowing down a little.

"It's not easy to cut yourself off from something you have been doing all your life," explains Augusta. "It would be very demoralising. I like to be involved and to keep busy and I actually enjoy the routine. I do the flowers and help serve in the restaurant. If I stopped doing that, what would I do with myself all day? I have my crochet, of course, but television doesn't interest me. And Lino would hate not being part of the restaurant. He loves people and he has so many friends among the customers, many of whom he has known for years. He loves being able to chat with them. For both of us, the restaurant is still very much part of our lives."

The day will come, of course, when Peter and Helen will take over the running of the restaurant completely. That has always been the plan and it gives Augusta and Lino a tremendous sense of satisfaction to know that the great family tradition that gives the *The Butcher's Arms* its very special character will be continued for at least one more generation, if not more.

With a view to their eventual retirement, they recently bought a bungalow in the village, demolished it and had it re-built to a luxurious standards. Once again, they relish the challenge of transforming the bare garden plot that surrounds it into a showpiece, using the horticultural skills they have developed over the years.

In 2005, more than 45 years after they arrived on these shores, Lino and Augusta made the decision to apply for British citizenship. To their astonishment – and alarm – their request was at first refused. Considering their impressive contribution to the country of their choice, not only in building up a successful business but also in working tirelessly for charity, and given also that they had been sponsored by such august figures as Lord Lawson, Lord Heseltine and Baroness Knight of Collingree, Lino and Augusta were naturally baffled as to why they should have been turned down.

Enquiries with the Home Office then revealed that they had never applied for 'indefinite leave to remain' in the U.K. It was a pure oversight, nobody having realised that such permission had to be applied for. Naturally enough, it led to the inevitable jokes amongst their friends about 'illegal immigrants'.

A year later they applied again and this time their long-held dream of becoming British citizens was finally granted. At an official ceremony in Warwick's Shire Hall on July 4th, 2006, Lino and Augusta swore allegiance to the Queen, sang a lusty and enthusiastic version of 'God Save The Queen' and were delighted when their naturalisation papers were finally handed over.

A few months later, on one of her regular visits to Portugal for a few days relaxation at the villa, Augusta was thrilled when she was able to use her British passport for the first time. "I felt wonderful and thought, 'Wow, I'm finally British', as I handed it over to the immigration official," she recalls. "And I when he spotted that it was my birthday and wished me 'Happy Birthday' I was even more excited."

Augusta has always admitted that for a while after leaving Portugal she had divided loyalties. "It was like having a Portuguese mother and an English father, and it left me never feeling certain about where I truly belonged," she explains. "But for many years now I have felt 100 per cent British. I love going back to Portugal, but my life is here. And my heart is here. Whenever I come back to Priors Hardwick after being away, I think: 'Oh, how wonderful, I'm home again'."

Augusta with sister Maria Santos (left) and Maria Marques.

Rosemarie Higham (Former Banbury Town Mayor, customer and friend):

....

❛ I adore Augusta's great kindness. She is so sincere, genuine and understanding.
She has a very homely, warm, motherly touch that we all love. But despite her love
of nice things, she never forgets her roots – that is what makes her so special.
Above all, she cares for you as an individual, not just as a customer, and that is an
amazing quality. I once remarked on her glorious perfume and said how much
I liked it. The next time I saw her, knowing I hadn't been well, she gave me a present
– a bottle of that lovely Valentino perfume. I was immensely touched. To remember
that sort of thing when she often has so much on her mind is extraordinary.

Both Augusta and Lino have poured their heart and soul into The Butcher's
Arms, and it shows. It doesn't matter who you take there, one thing you can be
sure of is that you will be greeted warmly, the food and wine will be very good and
you always know you are going to have a great time. ❜

....

David Hobbs (Former racing driver, longtime customer and friend):

....

' One of the fun things that I and my wife, Margaret, used to enjoy doing with Augusta and Lino from time to time when we were still living in the village was to take ourselves off for slap-up lunches at various different restaurants around England and Wales. The beauty of it was that there was something in it for each one of us. Lino, who always insisted on paying, was able to sample someone else's food and keep an eye on the opposition, Margaret got to choose which restaurant we would favour with our custom, I got to drive – and Augusta was thrilled because Lino wasn't driving. She always used to say that Lino was such a terrible driver that she would end up crying all the time whenever she was in a car with him. Mind you, Lino didn't like her driving – and I wouldn't have driven with either of them!

Over the years we had some memorable lunches in wonderful restaurants such as The Walnut Tree Inn, near Abergavenny, Simpsons in Edgbaston and Hintlesham Hall in Suffolk, which was then owned by one of the first celebrity chefs, Robert Carrier. It was the lunch at Hintlesham Hall that nearly proved to be our last. We were on the return journey, almost home and rocketing along the A361 at a rate of knots. As we came over the brow of a hill, we were suddenly faced with a line of stationary traffic in front of us. I put the car into a massive, racing-type braking situation and we slid to a halt just in time, missing the vehicle in front of us by inches.

At the same time as Lino was saying, 'Well done, Dave', Augusta was
screaming and almost fainting with fright in the back. I then glanced in the
mirror and, much to my alarm, saw another car come hurtling over the brow of
the hill towards us. I quickly reversed onto the verge and out of the way a
fraction of a second before the oncoming car, with its anchors full on, smacked
straight into the car that had been in front of us.

Once we were out of harm's way, Augusta visibly relaxed and began to praise
me for saving all our lives. Mind you, it must have also helped settle her
driving nerves because soon after that incident she went out and bought herself a
big white Porsche 928! **'**

Nuno Correia (Waiter):

....

' Augusta has been absolutely amazing to me. She has given me the most

fantastic opportunities – and I have huge respect for her because of this.

When I first arrived here I was told that one of the nicest things about

The Butcher's Arms is that you will feel part of the family and it is so true.

We all feel as if we belong and we do our very best for Augusta and Lino

because they have treated us so well. Because she is so sensitive,

and always concerned for other people, Augusta seems to have the ability

to read their minds. If you are miserable she will spot it straight away

and try and find out what is wrong.

When I lived next door to the restaurant, many times Augusta

would come round with some tomato rice. Even now, if she cooks

it for herself and Lino on a Saturday lunch time, if she has any

left over she will say: 'Oh, Nuno, I have some tomato rice for

you,' and I take it home to enjoy it later.

She and Lino are very kind and generous. They gave me

some money to buy my first car. And then they gave me my

wife Alison, who I met when she was a customer in the

restaurant, the opportunity to live in a house in the village.

What they do for other people is priceless. '

....

Edward Pires (Grandson, born 13 May 1993):

....

❛ I love my Nanny because she cares so much! Even when I don't see her that often
she is always there with a hug and a kind word. I am really interested to see
Nanny's book when it is finished. I bet it will be brilliant, just like her.
The only time I ever see her get cross is when she is speaking Portuguese with
Granddad or when James and I fight. ❜

....

James Pires (Grandson, born 24 May 1996):

....

❛ My Nanny is extremely helpful and generous and kind. She works and works
and works and even when people tell her to rest or have a
holiday she will not listen.She never seems to stop working
even when she is ill. It makes me shiver when I see her cry
but she always perks up in the end. She is very unlucky
with her illness but will always be there to help anyone.
It is stunning really. She is always kind, caring and
generous to everyone but never wants anyone to fuss over
her. I am very proud to be her grandson. ❜

....

Heather Pires (Granddaughter, born 30 May 1991):

. . . .

' Some of my earliest memories involve Nanny, from teaching her (in vain) how to send a text message, to visiting Paiágua with her and listening to stories from her childhood, including her immense fear of snakes.

Nanny is an emotional and giving person who has a wonderfully expressive and friendly laugh and her sensitivity and generosity never cease to amaze me. She has the kindest heart in existence. The trials and tribulations of her life have not knocked her and she has a tremendous ability to forgive people and not judge them too harshly. To many people, and of course that includes me, she is a joyous, loving and beautiful person. Being with her helps light up my days. Her accomplishments in life are astounding. Her whole life is a testament to how success can be achieved if you are determined and work hard. She is a true inspiration to me.

I am proud to tell people that my grandma is one of the most selfless, thoughtful people I know. She is always insisting that everyone else around her is more important than herself, which, of course, is not true. I hope this book shows her how much appreciated she is. My granddad and my brothers and I would be at a loss without her. '

. . . .

Helen Pires (Daughter-in-Law):

. . . .

❛ Augusta is an absolute perfectionist. She likes everything to be spot on, which is why things work and are always so consistent. She provides the link between the kitchen and the restaurant, keeping her eye on everything, on the ball the whole time.

She is also, as everybody knows, a fantastic cook.

Her whole family are natural cooks.

Augusta sees it as her job in life to feed all her family well. I've had some wonderful meals with her and Lino at their home. Her fish stew, particularly, is delicious. It's one of my favourite Augusta dishes. She always took great care to pick the best pieces of fish.

She is not the showman and not as confident as Lino. But she is a strong and determined woman, someone whom you cannot fail to admire. ❜

. . . .

Roger Puttnam (Former chairman of Ford UK and a regular customer
for over 25 years, seen here with Augusta and his wife, Trish):

❛ Augusta's great strength is that she is the hidden pillar behind Lino.
She sits in her little control room in the middle of the restaurant
and runs everything brilliantly.
No one would ever know she was there, but she is the one who makes
the wheels run smoothly.
For such a shy and retiring personality, it is amazing how resolute she is
and how strong. She is the rock on which the family and the restaurant
have stood over the years. ❜

Terry McGregor ('Trolley Dolly' in charge of the sweet trolley
at The Butcher's Arms for longer than she cares to remember!):
....

❛ Augusta is such a good, natural cook that I only have to look at a dessert and I know instantly whether it has been made by the chef or Augusta. She has this amazing light, feathery touch, whatever dish she is making.

The wonderful thing about Lino and Augusta is that they treat all their employees like their family. We all appreciate that. I have worked for them for 28 years and it has never been a question of bosses and workers with them. And they never tell you to do something, they ask you. And that means so much.

We all know Augusta has a very warm heart and can never do enough for people. Although she is very shy, she is also loyal, loving and sympathetic – and emotional. When Christmas comes and the carol singers come into the restaurant the tears always flow. I'm used to it now, I always jokingly say, 'Oh, come on now, stop it!' and then that wonderful smile appears.

Without Augusta, Lino's life could have been very different. He now has everything he'd always wanted, simply because of Augusta. She has always been there supporting him, whatever he wanted to do. If he wanted to take a risk, even if she was worried or unsure about it, she would put his wishes first and support him all the way. They think the world of each other. ❜

....

Sir Nick Scheele (Former Chairman and CEO of Jaguar, Chairman of Ford Europe and President and Chief Operating Officer of Ford in America and a regular customer and friend):

....

❛ *I always describe Lino as the best 'mine host' in the world. And Augusta is just a shining angel – she sparkles. She's always there and she's always incredibly cheerful. Together, she and Lino are an amazing couple.*

"I first started going to The Butcher's Arms in 1991. I had been working for Ford in Mexico and had just been invited to take over at Jaguar. I came over to look for a house and a school for our youngest and the Jaguar people took me and my wife to dinner at The Butcher's Arms. We sat at the big round table and had the most wonderful evening and it has been my favourite restaurant in the world ever since.

"Although she calls Lino 'Boss', it is Augusta who is quietly running things behind the scenes. And how brilliantly she does it! My eldest son's wedding reception was held at The Butcher's Arms. We filled the place and were offered six main course selections – and yet everybody was served at exactly the same time. It was quite stunning.

"Although we have been living in the US since I moved over there to become Group Vice President with Ford North America in 2001, we still have a place in this country and we go to The Butcher's Arms whenever we are over here. It is not only our favourite restaurant, it is also our children's favourite and even the grandchildren have started going there now. They love it because Augusta makes such a fuss of them. ❜

....

John Bowe (Actor and longtime customer):

‘ Augusta is quite simply 'Mother Earth'! If I had been orphaned as a child I would have chosen Augusta for my mother. She is the warmest and most loving of human beings and her love of children and babies is unceasing. Emma and I well remember our wedding in Priors Hardwick and the fantastic reception and dinner that we all had at The Butcher's Arms. As always Lino and Augusta spoilt us and all our guests, family and friends. Maddie, our eldest daughter, was only nine months old at the time and so that Emma could enjoy her wedding, her food, wine and friends, Augusta, on more than one occasion, took Maddie in her arms and disappeared with her.

At one point I did ask Emma if she thought we would ever see our little daughter again. But the fact is that had we lost her to Augusta, I know that she would have had the most magical life, filled with the very best of happiness and love. This is the mark of the woman. She is 'love'. ’

Harry Rhodes (Photographer, customer and friend):

‧‧

❛ *Augusta is always so concerned that people are well looked after. One day I was doing some photography at The Butcher's Arms accompanied by an acquaintance and at the end of the session we chatted to Peter, who then kindly offered us a glass of wine. Shortly afterwards we were in the car park, happily eating some sandwiches we'd brought with us, when Augusta appeared with Figo, the dog, and a large bucket of bread that she was going to feed to the birds. When she asked why we weren't eating in the restaurant I jokingly told her that Peter wouldn't serve us, so we were forced to eat sandwiches in the car park, which of course wasn't at all true. The next thing I knew, she'd found Peter and was giving him a severe telling off for not giving us lunch. The poor chap, who hadn't done anything wrong, didn't know what had hit him!* ❜

‧‧

Professor David Cunningham
(The consultant at the Royal Marsden Hospital who treated both Augusta and Peter.
The profits from the sale of this book will go to his Research Fund.)

....

' In a way, it is almost impossible to separate Augusta and Lino because they live their life as a team – a team that has been incredibly successful in building one of the finest restaurant businesses in the United Kingdom. More than this, they have created a warm, wonderful family, who show enormous love and consideration towards others. However, within the partnership Augusta shows great sensitivity and emotional strengths coupled with superb people skills and a real ability to make everyone feel extremely special. Even in her darkest moments, she never fails to think about other people. She also has superb 'artistic' skills, including embroidery, weaving and crochet. My wife and I are proud to possess some of her finest creations, which are really works of art. Augusta has undoubtedly given more to life than she has taken and the world is a better place for her being here. '

....

Butcher's Arms Fishcakes

This is one of our most popular dishes.

MAKES 10 FISHCAKES
2 lb/ 900g fresh salmon
   (de-boned and skinned)
1 lb/450g natural smoked haddock
4 oz/115g prawns
2 eggs (hardboiled – chopped finely)
1 egg (beaten)
1 tablespoon chopped parsley
½ pint/300ml milk
1½ oz/40g plain flour
1½ oz/40g butter
freshly grated nutmeg
breadcrumbs
salt and freshly ground black pepper

GRAIN MUSTARD SAUCE
1 pint/600ml dry white wine
1 oz/30g butter
1 oz/30g flour
1 tablespoon grain mustard
1 egg yolk
double cream
salt and pepper

Fishcakes

Poach the salmon in salted water and make sure it doesn't cook longer than is necessary otherwise it will be dry (takes approx. five minutes). Remove skin and bones. Drain the salmon in a colander. Do the same with the natural smoked haddock. Finally cook the prawns (they only need warming up if you use frozen cooked ones but remember you can't expect a good result if you use anything other than first class produce).

Mix the fish and prawns together in a bowl with the hardboiled eggs and a tablespoon of chopped parsley.

To bind this together you need to make a very thick white sauce from the milk, flour and butter.

Melt the butter gently and add the flour. When this is fully absorbed pour in the milk and stir vigorously to prevent burning. Add the fish and let the mixture boil gently for a minute and then remove from the heat. Season the mixture to taste with pepper, salt and freshly grated nutmeg.

Let the mixture cool down in the fridge. When cold divide into 10 equal portions and roll into seamless balls. Roll each ball through the flour, beaten egg and breadcrumbs and then press firmly into a 2″ diameter biscuit cutter.

You can freeze the fishcakes or cook them from fresh in a medium hot fryer. Serve with mustard sauce.

Grain Mustard Sauce

Melt butter and add the flour. Then add 1 pint of white wine, stirring all the time. Bring slowly to the boil and add one large tablespoon of grain mustard. Season with salt and pepper and finish by adding 1 egg yolk mixed with some double cream.

Note: *Do not let the sauce boil after you have added the egg yolk.*

Langoustines in Garlic Butter

Angelo and Pepe were a lovely married couple and two of the best waiters we ever had in The Butchers Arms. Pepe had a lovely smile and was a great communiciator, the customers loved her. When they were working here she became pregnant with triplets and I will never forget Angelo's face when he received the news in a telephone call when he was working in the kitchen. He went white. Some years later Angelo and Pepe returned with their beautiful teenage triplets to visit.

It was Angelo who was responsible for introducing langoustines to the menu. Lino visited him one Christmas Day while he was cooking them for lunch. When Lino expressed interest in putting them on The Butchers Arms menu, Angelo said that if he did then Lino would never forget him because once the customers tasted them they would be on the menu forever. He was absolutely right. It has also been our most profitable dish ever!

SERVES 4

20 raw, shell-on large tiger prawns or 24 langoustines

4 cloves of garlic, peeled and crushed

3 oz/75g butter, softened

1 heaped tablespoon chopped fresh parsley

grated zest and juice ½ lemon

salt and freshly milled black pepper

chopped fresh parsley

1 lemon, quartered

To butterfly the prawns, first of all pull off the heads and legs with your fingers, then simply peel away the shells, which come away very easily, but leave the tails still attached, as this makes them look prettier.

Now turn each prawn on its back and, with the point of a sharp knife, make a cut down the centre of each prawn, but do not cut through. Ease open with your thumb like a

*Augusta and Lino with husband-and-wife waiters Pepe (left) and Angelo (back right)
and their beautiful triplet daughters.*

book and remove the brownish-black thread, scraping it away with the point of the knife –
it should also come away easily. Next rinse the prawns and pat them dry with kitchen
paper, then place them in the buttered gratin dishes or on the baking tray.

Next make the garlic butter by taking a large fork and combining the rest of the
ingredients together in a bowl. Spread equal quantities of the garlic butter over the
prawns. To cook the prawns, pre-heat the oven to gas mark 8, 450F (230C), and place the
dishes on the highest shelf of the oven and let them cook for 6–7 minutes. Serve sprinkled
with the parsley and garnish with the lemon quarters.

Goujons of Plaice

"My first job in the kitchens was preparing the plaice for the goujons, a job that always left me smelling of fish for ages afterwards," recalls celebrity chef Tony Tobin of his early days at the The Butcher's Arms. "This was an incredibly popular dish, they would almost fly out of the kitchen door! I'm not surprised it was Lord Heseltine's favourite starter."

> fillets of plaice
> beaten egg
> milk
> flour
> breadcrumbs
> oil for frying

Remove the skin from the fillets and trim off the outside fins. If the fillet was a cross cut, make sure you remove the centre as this contains cartilage.

Cut the fillets into strips the size of a large finger. Dip them into flour and then into a mixture of beaten egg and milk. Cover with breadcrumbs making sure they are well covered and fry in a medium hot deep fat fryer.

Serve with a generous wedge of lemon and tartare sauce.

Molotov

As Terry, our 'trolley dolly', will confirm, this Portuguese dish is one of the most popular sweets.

MOLOTOV
14 egg whites
14 dessertspoons of caster sugar
golden syrup
water

CUSTARD SAUCE
14 egg yolks
14 dessertspoons caster sugar
7 fl oz/200ml water

A 12 – 14 inch angel cake mould (a round mould with a hole in the centre)

Whisk the egg whites in a grease free bowl until they are light and fluffy. Add the caster sugar and enough golden syrup to get a light brown colour. Grease the mould with butter and pour in the mixture, making sure there are no spaces.

Put in the oven in a bain marie (a roasting tin with enough water to come halfway up the sides of the mould) and bake for 15 minutes at 175 C.

Turn the oven off and leave the pudding inside for a further 15 minutes

To make the custard sauce
Put the egg yolks in a saucepan with the sugar and water and cook until it curdles a little bit and then whisk. Leave to cool. Take the pudding out of the oven, loosen the sides with a spatula or knife and place a plate over the top. Turn the plate and mould over gently. The pudding should slide out. Pour the custard sauce over the top and serve.

Acknowledgements

Live Wire Books would like to thank the following:

All friends, colleagues and family members who have kindly taken the trouble to contribute their thoughts and photographs.

Vitor Tomé, from Castelo Branco for his invaluable research in Portugal.

Nuno Correia for help with translation.

Alberto Simao for the photographs on pages 12 and 29.

Photograph of Westgate Arms, Warwick on page 110 reproduced by kind permission of Iliffe News and Media.

Photographs on pages 122, 127, 131, 132, 133, 135, 168, 169, 171, 196, 201, 206, 209 and 224 by Harry Rhodes, Tudor Photography, Banbury.

Photograph on page 114 reproduced by kind permission of Rugby School.

Photographs on page 60, 64, 68 and 81 courtesy of the Portuguese Tourist Board.

Photographs on pages 37, 75, 76, 96, 116 and 187 courtesy of iStockphoto.

Photograph on page 93 courtesy of The Leicester Mercury.

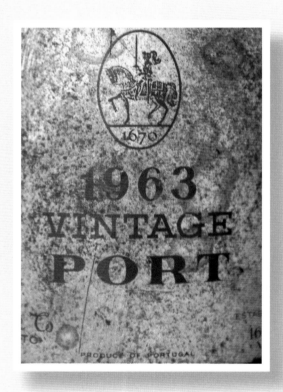